SUCCESSFUL ACTIVITIES FOR ENRICHING THE LANGUAGE ARTS

Betty Coody

Lamar University

David Nelson

Saginaw Valley State University

WAVELAND
PRESS, INC.

Prospect Heights, Illinois

For information about this book, write or call:

Waveland Press, Inc.
P.O. Box 400
Prospect Heights, Illinois 60070
(708) 634-0081

Acknowledgments: Map of the United States of America is from *Rand McNally Cosmopolitan World Atlas*, 1976. Copyright © by Rand McNally & Company.

Also by the same authors and available from Waveland Press, Inc.
TEACHING ELEMENTARY LANGUAGE ARTS: A Literature Approach

TABLE OF CONTENTS

Part III.　Activities to Enrich Grammar and Spelling　99

Part IV.　Activities to Enrich Speaking　133

Part V.　Activities to Enrich Listening　151

Memory Mandala   161
Manual Alphabet   163

Part VI.   Activities to Enrich Literature and Library Programs   167

Reading Record Chart   167
Dial-a-Book   171
Colorful Classifications   174
Dewey Decimal Scavenger Hunt   176
Card Catalog Clue   179
"Stained Glass" Book Reports   182
Student-Made Slides   184
Caldecott Bingo   187
Newbery Bingo   196

Appendix A.   Dolch Basic Sight Word List   209
Appendix B.   Frequently Used Nouns   211
Appendix C.   Word Families For Substitution of Initial Consonant Sounds   212
Appendix D.   Prefixes   215
Appendix E.   Suffixes   217
Appendix F.   Compound Words   218
Appendix G.   Contractions   221
Appendix H.   Common Abbreviations   222
Appendix I.   Antonyms   225
Appendix J.   Homophones   227
Appendix K.   Rhyming Words   229
Appendix L.   Popular Acronyms   236
Appendix M.   Wilson's Essential Vocabulary   237
Appendix N.   Books for Reading Aloud to Primary Children   241
Appendix O.   Books for Reading Aloud to Third and Fourth Graders   243
Appendix P.   Great Quotations on Books and Reading   245
Appendix Q.   One Hundred Creative Alternatives to Written Book Reports   247
Appendix R.   The Caldecott Award Books   250
Appendix S.   The Newbery Award Books   252
Appendix T.   Publishers' Addresses   254

PREFACE

This book provides elementary language arts teachers with an array of activities designed to enrich the reading, writing, speaking, and listening skills of their students. The activities and materials have been tested with students in many classrooms and have been altered and modified according to suggestions from both students and teachers.

The book is intended as a supplement to regular textbooks in language arts courses at both the graduate and undergraduate levels. Teachers in service will find the activities practical, pertinent, and convenient to use at once with their students. Preservice teachers, on the other hand, will be able to learn the important skills of planning, developing, and evaluating independent activities for children.

We wish to express our gratitude to the people who helped in the preparation of this book. Karen Sanders not only typed the manuscript, but assisted in organizing, editing, duplicating, and all the other (some not-so-professional) tasks we sent her way. Barbara Ellis is a talented artist, as her drawings reveal; but her training in teacher education and her experience in the classroom were of equal value to us. She was able to look at our stick drawings and understand what we were trying to show. Any person using this book will appreciate her careful work.

Our spouses, Carol Nelson and H. L. Coody, have helped us in countless ways. They were patient and supportive when we were forced to work through family vacations, weekends, and finally holidays.

We would like to thank Professor Mary H. Appleberry of the Stephen F. Austin State University in Nacogdoches, Texas, for generously evaluating and critiquing the primary draft of the manuscript. We found her comments most helpful.

A special debt of gratitude is owed to our college students and to our colleagues in the public schools. Their ideas and suggestions are reflected in each one of the activities we describe in this book.

Betty Coody
David Nelson

HOW THIS BOOK IS ORGANIZED

The major purpose of *Successful Activities to Enrich the Language Arts* is to offer elementary students interesting ways to practice language arts skills. Efficient and fluent use of the skills of reading, writing, listening, and speaking depends almost entirely on the amount of meaningful practice that students experience during the formative years.

It is relatively easy for teachers to provide activities that entertain children and occupy their spare time; but to find activities that actually strengthen and improve skills at the same time is a much more difficult task. This handbook is designed to meet an obvious need for independent activities of quality and substance to enrich and extend language arts instruction.

Although fewer activities will be presented in detail than are to be found in other activity books, each activity is comprehensive and will provide the teacher with an effective, durable teaching tool that can be used with many students over a period of years.

A survey of both graduate and undergraduate students studying elementary education revealed certain features that are preferred in an activity book; and these students' ideas were used in the development of these activities. Based on teacher recommendations, the activities are designed as follows:

1. *Each activity or game is designed to strengthen a specific language arts skill.* Although most activities pertain to more than one skill, a single one has been isolated for special emphasis. The skill area is conveniently designated for the benefit of the teacher who is seeking an audiovisual aid to help correct a particular difficulty. All activities are cross-referenced to the skills being reinforced.

2. *The major purposes and objectives of each activity are clearly and concisely stated.* Teachers want to know what the activity purports to teach and what outcomes can be expected. The use of independent activities, in a game format, can be defended to parents and administrators if it is shown that both cognitive learning and skill development are built into these activities.

3. *Lucid step-by-step directions are given for directing activities and constructing games.* Because a consistent formula style of writing is used for each activity, teachers and aides will become accustomed to referring to certain places for the specific information needed. Descriptive passages are abbreviated and illustrated to conserve teacher time and energy.

4. *Instructions for carrying out an activity or playing a game are written simply and accurately so that students can read and follow them without a disproportionate amount of help from the teacher.* Because all directions to be read by students are placed in a boxed insert, the teacher will find it easy to enlarge the information to chart size or otherwise duplicate it for students to read until the activity becomes familiar. Clear instructions accompanying each activity make it possible for students to be more independent, thus freeing the teacher for other tasks.

5. *A "shopping list" of all the materials needed for constructing an aid is provided at the outset.* Teachers want to know approximately how much the raw materials for a teaching device will cost, where to find the materials, the dimensions needed, and other vital purchasing information. There are also suggestions for ways to use free and inexpensive scrap materials in making games and audiovisual aids.

6. *The teaching aids are versatile enough to appeal to children of various age and ability levels and to those of different ethnic and language backgrounds.* Language arts activities need to be challenging to all levels of achievement in order that students may progress from one to the other over a period of time. A convenient coding system provided for the teacher's benefit indicates the different levels of difficulty. In some instances, suggestions have been given for simplifying an activity or for making it more challenging.

7. *The activities are varied enough to provide for different class-grouping arrangements.* Some activities have been planned for groups as large as the entire class, whereas others are more suitable for small groups, teams of two, or individual students. The description of each activity includes the number of participants required or the number it will accommodate.

8. *Materials are designed with eye appeal to motivate and stimulate students to practice.* Teachers appreciate directions and suggestions

for making visual aids that are attractive, colorful, sturdy, and durable. Appropriate line drawings in this activity book help to clarify instructions and give an idea of what the finished product will look like.

9. *Actual contents for teacher-made activities are included in the handbook.* A rather exhaustive set of appendices includes frequently used sight words, common nouns, proper nouns, compound words, prefixes, suffixes, homonyms, synonyms, antonyms, abbreviations, contractions, and so forth. These lists will supplement basal textbook content used at various grade levels and will be useful in making all kinds of games and activities.

10. *Each activity is accompanied by a plan for informal evaluation.* Teachers want to know if the routine use of independent activities actually does improve the reading, writing, speaking, and listening skills of students. In this book are specific suggestions for quick appraisal to determine whether or not objectives are being met.

11. *Suggestions are given for displaying the activities, games, and devices to make them convenient for teachers and students.* The best methods of organizing, filing, and storing materials for easy access are recommended and illustrated—from drawstring bags to pocket folders. Practical ideas are given for conserving as much classroom space as possible.

Because most language arts teachers operate on some form of sequential skills continuum, this activity book is carefully cross-referenced to the skills and sub-skills each activity reinforces. Such an arrangement makes each section equivalent to a lesson plan for individualized instruction.

FORMAT OF EACH ACTIVITY

    I. Title

    II. Brief description with line drawing

    III. Purposes and objectives

    IV. Number of players or participants

    V. Materials needed

    VI. Instructions for making aid

    VII. Student directions

    VIII. Variations and teaching hints

    IX. Display and storage

    X. Evaluation

Criteria For Teacher-Made Games

Experience has shown that it is necessary to observe certain criteria in constructing learning activities and games for successful classroom use. Learning activities and games should be—

1. *purposeful.* A game should provide needed practice, preferably review. The purpose of the activity should be clearly understood by both the teacher and the children.

2. *attractive.* Game materials and their storage boxes or containers should be bright and colorful.

3. *flexible.* The basic components of the game should be constructed so that they can be utilized not only for reading but for other subjects as well, for example, mathematics and science. Students at various levels of ability should be able to participate in the games.

4. *sturdy.* Materials and designs should be chosen to withstand several months or years of normal wear and tear.

5. *appropriate.* Decisions concerning materials, design, directions, and format should be made on the basis of the particular characteristics of the group for which the game is intended. Many factors should be considered, such as the age of the children, their present academic achievement, their previous experience with games, the size of the group, the furniture within the classroom, the amount of space available for playing the game, and the skill or subject the game is intended to reinforce.

6. *clear and uncomplicated.* Clarity in oral and written directions is essential. Labels, diagrams, and simple directions on game storage containers are recommended. Playing procedures should be uncomplicated, and an initial demonstration involving the teacher and students is indispensable. It is suggested that the teacher play a trial run before bringing the game into the classroom.

7. *self-checking and correcting.* The game should allow for help to be given and received among students. If checksheets are necessary, they should be included as part of the game package. The game should be designed so that once the children are familiar with the playing procedure, they can be generally independent of teacher supervision.

8. *designed for use by small groups of players.* Two to four students generally constitute a smoothly working, harmonious group. Larger groups cause participants to spend too much time awaiting a turn and too little time actually playing and receiving practice. The construction of multiple sets of a game allows children to play the game in small groups.

PAGE	ACTIVITY	GRADE LEVEL			BASIC SKILLS AREA EMPHASIZED						SUITABILITY FOR SPECIAL CHILDREN		
		PRIMARY (K–2)	INTERMEDIATE (3,4)	UPPER ELEMENTARY (5,6)	READING	WRITING	GRAMMAR/SPELLING	SPEAKING	LISTENING	LIBRARY/LITERATURE	BILINGUAL	MAINSTREAMED	ACCELERATED
53	Alligator Bog Map Skills		X		X								
91	Berry Ink and Quill Pen		X	X		X							X
14	Bleach Bottle Tachistoscope	X			X						X		
83	Bookbinding			X		X							
51	Browse Boxes		X	X	X						X		
187	Caldecott Bingo		X							X			X
158	Canned Consonants	X							X			X	
124	Car Capers			X				X				X	X
179	Card Catalog Clue			X						X			X
107	Chief Spellum Chart	X					X						
63	Chinese Tangrams		X	X		X							X
133	Classroom Cookery	X							X		X	X	X
5	Cloze Lines		X		X						X		
70	Collection Compositions			X		X							X
174	Colorful Classifications			X						X			X
24	Compound Concentration		X		X								

PAGE	ACTIVITY	GRADE LEVEL			BASIC SKILLS AREA EMPHASIZED						SUITABILITY FOR SPECIAL CHILDREN		
		PRIMARY (K–2)	INTERMEDIATE (3,4)	UPPER ELEMENTARY (5,6)	READING	WRITING	GRAMMAR/SPELLING	SPEAKING	LISTENING	LIBRARY/LITERATURE	BILINGUAL	MAINSTREAMED	ACCELERATED
128	Crossword Puzzles		×				×						×
176	Dewey Decimal Scavenger Hunt		×							×			×
171	Dial-a-Book			×						×			×
137	Earth, Sea, and Sky Frieze	×						×			×	×	
144	Felt Books	×						×				×	
43	Four-Fold Quiz		×		×								
122	Grammar "500"		×	×			×				×		
111	Holiday Vocabulary Charts	×					×				×	×	
22	Homophone Hunt	×			×		×					×	
139	Jigsaw Puzzles	×			×			×				×	
80	Lively Limericks			×		×		×					×
151	Lucy the Listener	×							×			×	
36	The Magic Key	×			×						×		
163	Manual Alphabet	×	×						×		×	×	
75	Mask Makers			×		×					×		
161	Memory Mandala	×								×	×	×	

		GRADE LEVEL			BASIC SKILLS AREA EMPHASIZED						SUITABILITY FOR SPECIAL CHILDREN		
PAGE	ACTIVITY	PRIMARY (K–2)	INTERMEDIATE (3,4)	UPPER ELEMENTARY (5,6)	READING	WRITING	GRAMMAR/SPELLING	SPEAKING	LISTENING	LIBRARY/LITERATURE	BILINGUAL	MAINSTREAMED	ACCELERATED
146	Milk Carton Puppets		X	X				X					X
141	Moody Jack-O'-Lanterns	X						X				X	
96	Multipurpose Board	X				X						X	
1	Name That Symbol		X		X								
196	Newbery Bingo			X						X			X
41	Newspaper Art		X		X								
104	Noun House	X					X				X		
117	Noun Password	X	X				X						
93	On Your Punctuation Mark		X	X		X							
102	Paper Folding	X						X					X
73	Picture Postcards			X		X							X
78	Picture the Difference		X			X							
47	Propaganda Detective			X	X								X
148	Puppet Stages		X	X				X					X
39	The Question Box			X	X								X
8	Readers Theatre	X			X							X	

PAGE	ACTIVITY	GRADE LEVEL			BASIC SKILLS AREA EMPHASIZED						SUITABILITY FOR SPECIAL CHILDREN		
		PRIMARY (K–2)	INTERMEDIATE (3,4)	UPPER ELEMENTARY (5,6)	READING	WRITING	GRAMMAR/SPELLING	SPEAKING	LISTENING	LIBRARY/LITERATURE	BILINGUAL	MAINSTREAMED	ACCELERATED
167	Reading Record Chart	X	X							X	X	X	X
57	Road Map Reading			X	X						X		
12	Seasonal T-Scopes	X			X								
114	Sentence Building Blocks	X					X				X		X
68	Shape Books	X				X							
20	Sight Word Bingo	X			X								
160	Sound Barrels and Boxes	X							X			X	
154	Sound Bingo	X							X			X	
109	Spelling Progress Chart		X				X				X		
17	Sports Lingo		X		X								
182	"Stained Glass" Book Reports	X	X							X			
156	Story Murals	X	X						X				
184	Student-Made Slides			X						X			X
119	Syllaboat Sail		X	X			X						X
45	Trademark Montage	X			X								
99	A Tree for All Seasons	X					X						

		GRADE LEVEL			BASIC SKILLS AREA EMPHASIZED						SUITABILITY FOR SPECIAL CHILDREN		
PAGE	ACTIVITY	PRIMARY (K–2)	INTERMEDIATE (3,4)	UPPER ELEMENTARY (5,6)	READING	WRITING	GRAMMAR/SPELLING	SPEAKING	LISTENING	LIBRARY/LITERATURE	BILINGUAL	MAINSTREAMED	ACCELERATED
31	Word Checkers	X			X								
26	Word Dominoes	X	X		X								
87	Writing: It's in the Bag		X	X		X							
66	Writing Trifolders	X				X					X		
33	Yes-No-Maybe Boxes	X			X								

PART I

ACTIVITIES TO ENRICH READING

Name That Symbol

Children are surrounded by symbols and signs of all kinds—signs that are used as a visual shorthand for countless concepts, philosophies, services, and products. Students need to learn as many of these symbols as possible and to understand them as a form of communication. To be able to respond accurately to symbols is a literacy skill that is very important to students during school years and in later life as well.

Purposes and Objectives

1. To create an awareness of visual symbols in the environment
2. To teach the meaning of a variety of symbols
3. To develop a lasting curiosity about the origin and meaning of symbols

Number of Participants

Four

Materials Needed

- [ ] Two packs of 3″ × 5″ index cards
- [ ] Collection of popular symbols and accompanying definitions
- [ ] Scissors
- [ ] Paste

Instructions for Making Aid

Draw or cut out symbols of all kinds to paste on the playing cards. Signs that are useful to know may be found in magazines and papers, driver manuals, labels in the pantry, and countless other places. An excellent source for both you and your students is *Symbols and Their Meaning* by Rolf Myller (New York: Atheneum, 1980).

The twenty symbols in the illustration may serve as the nucleus of a symbol collection, but the collection should be ongoing with both you and your students adding to it over a period of time.

Once an ample collection of symbols has been accumulated, each one should be pasted on a separate card. Type a title, definition, and related facts about each symbol on other cards to be matched by students in the Name That Symbol card game.

STUDENT DIRECTIONS

1. Assemble four players.

2. Place symbol cards in a stack facedown on the table.

3. Place definition cards in a stack facedown on the table.

4. Take turns drawing a card from each stack until all cards are drawn.

5. The player who has the most matching pairs (symbol with its definition) is the winner.

Variations and Teaching Hints

This card game is a good supplement to Trademark Montage on page 46 and Alligator Bog on page 55.

Storage

Store in game center for student selection.

Evaluation

After the game has been in use for several weeks, use the symbol cards as flashcards and have students give either oral or written responses. This will help you to determine how many symbols have been learned and how well they are understood.

KEY TO "NAME THAT SYMBOL"

1. The arrow has been used to symbolize direction since primitive people shot arrows at a target. The arrow symbol is related to pointing with the finger, which is one of the first symbols understood and used by infants.

2. The dove's footprint is a symbol for peace and, also, for nuclear disarmament.

3. The ace of spades is a symbol in playing cards. It is believed by some to be a bad luck omen.

4. In all parts of the world, the skull and crossbones represents poison, death, and danger. As a popular symbol of Halloween, the skull and crossbones is connected with the pagan belief that skeletons emerged from the grave on Halloween.

5. An old Chinese symbol called *yin and yang*. It represents two opposing forces combined to create unity, as day and night, hot and cold, and represent blood and bandages.

6. Crossed slash marks stand for *NO* and *DON'T*. It is a very bold and dramatic symbol that makes everyone take notice that something is forbidden.

7. The logo in the illustration is the registered trademark of the Mercedes-Benz automobile. Each automobile make has its own special logo.

8. The symbol for *female* was first used as a biological label for plants and animals. This symbol is said to be in the shape of a hand mirror that might have been used by a woman.

9. The symbol for *male* was first used as a biological label for plants and animals. This symbol is said to be in the shape of an arrow that might have been shot by a man.

10. The caduceus, a snake coiled around a walking stick, represents the medical profession. This symbol is associated with doctors of ancient Greece, who believed that snakes possessed healing powers.

11. A bent arrow tells traffic which way to turn, but with a slash mark across it, it means *no turn*. In the illustration, the combined symbols mean *no right turn*.

12. A red and white striped pole indicates a barber shop. Because barbers at one time also performed surgery, the colors red and white represent blood and bandages.

How many of these symbols do you know?

 1

 2

 3

 4

 5

 6

 7

 8

 9

 10

 11

 12

 13

 14

 15

 16

 17

 18

 19

 20

13. The Christian cross symbolizes the crucifixion of Christ. Many churches are marked by a cross as are the tombstones of Christians.

14. A heart shape always represents love and affection. It is a popular symbol year-round, but even more so on Valentine's Day.

15. The universal symbol for *lost and found* is used in airports and terminals.

16. The swastika was once used by Greeks as a popular decoration for their architecture. During World War II, this symbol came to be used by the German Nazi party.

17. Taurus (the bull) is one of the twelve signs of the zodiac in astrology. Astrology had its beginning with the ancient belief that the positions of the stars influence human behavior.

18. The Star of David is a symbol of Judaism and it is believed to have been the coat of arms that King David wore on his shield into battle.

19. The ankh is a type of cross that was cherished by ancient Egyptians. It is a symbol for eternity.

20. The star is the symbol for the Dallas Cowboys, a popular professional football team from Texas. The emblem on the helmet stands for the *Lone Star of Texas*.

Cloze Lines

The *cloze* procedure is based on the gestalt principle of psychology that a person visualizes the whole after contemplating a part; the word "cloze" is derived from the concept of *closure*. A cloze test assumes that the ability to fill in blanks accurately in reading material is an indication of a reader's comprehension of that material.

The cloze procedure may be adapted for use as a teaching tool in reading instruction and is used in this activity in conjunction with the language experience approach. Group stories are dictated by students and recorded on a chart by the teacher. Later every fifth word is covered with a flap to be filled in by students as they read. Proper names should not be covered. To check the accuracy of responses, students simply lift the flap. The more accurate the decisions, the higher the comprehension.

Purposes and Objectives

1. To improve reading comprehension
2. To increase the ability to use context clues as an aid in reading

Cloze Lines

Fire Prevention Week: The Fire Triangle

Yesterday, October 12, Captain Brown came to talk to us. He told about fires ▨ how to prevent them. ▨ showed us the fire ▨. He said you need ▨ things for fire to ▨. Air, heat and fuel ▨ a fire. He told if we took off one of those three, the ▨ would die.

Captain Brown showed us ▨ classes of fires. Class A ▨ paper, cloth, wood or ▨ solid. Class B contains oil, ▨, gasoline, and other flammable ▨. Class C fires are electrical.

Number of Participants

Small groups

Materials Needed

- ☐ Chart paper
- ☐ Black felt-point pen
- ☐ Construction paper
- ☐ Masking tape
- ☐ Scissors

Instructions for Making Aid

Record on a chart the children's discussion of an interesting experience. Leaving the first and last sentences intact, cover every fifth word with a flap made of construction paper and fastened at the top with masking tape as shown in the illustration. As students read the chart, ask them to determine the word hidden from view. They should be encouraged to read ahead for meaning and then to think of a word that would make sense in the space; in other words, they are to *close* the space mentally.

Fire Prevention Week: The Fire Triangle

Yesterday, October 12, Captain Brown came to talk to us. He told about fires and how to prevent them. He showed us the fire triangle. He said you need three things for fire to burn. Air, heat and fuel make a fire. He told us if we took off one of those three, the fire would die.

Captain Brown showed us three classes of fires. Class A contains paper, cloth, wood or any solid. Class B contains oil, chemicals, gasoline, and other flammable liquids. Class C fires are electrical.

When the chart has been read, the student should check the accuracy of each judgment. If the exact word is not used, only a very close synonym should be accepted. On discussing the choices, students soon become aware that comprehension is adversely affected by the wrong use of a word.

Variations and Teaching Hints

This activity is excellent to use with students who are studying English as a second language. Because students help to compose the chart, the language is on their level of achievement and within their range of interests.

Display and Storage

As with other experience charts, these should be hung on a chart rack for rereading over a period of time.

Evaluation

1. Observable improvement in using context clues to decode words
2. Greater accuracy on reading-comprehension tests.

Readers Theatre

Readers theatre brings a new vitality to oral reading by giving students a chance to read dialogue before an audience. Because several students read parts in turn, readers theatre is often called *group reading*. Emphasis is placed on the literature and not on costumes, properties, or acting.

The script for a readers theatre performance is prepared by rewriting a story to create an emphasis on dialogue. Each character's speech is labeled with a code (see Readers Theatre Script). Descriptive passages are condensed and assigned to a narrator. It is the narrator who introduces the characters and sets the mood for the performance. The children who are to read should either sit or stand before the audience and hold their scripts in a relaxed fashion.

Purposes and Objectives

1. To gain practice in oral reading
2. To experience performing before an audience
3. To become familiar with folk literature

Number of Participants

Any number, depending on the number of characters in the play. Audience may consist of small group or the entire class.

Materials Needed

☐ Copy of a folk tale that contains a great deal of dialogue
☐ Colored markers
☐ Colored construction paper
☐ Typing paper
☐ Typewriter

Instructions for Making Aid

1. Convert the story into a script.
2. Type one copy of the script.
3. Duplicate one copy for each character represented.
4. Underline the first character's part with a colored marker to make it easier for the reader to follow.
5. Staple the marked copy on construction paper that is the same color as the underlining. Fold the mounted script in half.
6. Label the completed folder with name of the character.

7. Continue marking each character's lines with a different color.

8. Continue mounting each script on the same color used to underline the character's dialogue.

9. Continue labeling each completed folder with name of the character represented. On completion, there will be a separate colored folder for each character in the play.

10. Place folders together in a large brown envelope. Print the name of the play on the front and indicate the number of characters represented. The play is ready for readers theatre performances.

STUDENT DIRECTIONS

1. Select a script for reading.

2. Assign parts to your classmates.

3. Practice reading the play several times.

4. Read your play to the class.

Variations and Teaching Hints

Prepare scripts from several easy-to-read stories, such as "The Three Little Pigs," "The Three Bears," and "The Breman Town Musicians." Allow time for groups to practice reading the scripts.

Scripts may be used over and over for years by different readers. By selecting literature to fit the ability and interest level of each group, you can use readers theatre at all grade levels.

Storage

Store the folders in a file box for student access.

Evaluation

1. Improved oral reading
2. More attentive listening
3. Increased awareness of literature types
4. Greater skill in writing dialogue

Readers Theatre Script

The Story of the Three Little Pigs

N — Narrator
Pig 1 — First Little Pig
Pig 2 — Second Little Pig
Pig 3 — Third Little Pig
BBW — Big Bad Wolf

N.   Once upon a time there were three little pigs who went out into the world to seek their fortune. The first little pig met a man with a load of straw and said to him,

PIG 1.   Please, man, give me that straw to build me a house.

N.   Which the man did, and the little pig built a house with it. Soon along came the big bad wolf, who knocked on the door and said,

BBW.   Little pig, little pig,
Let me come in.
Or I'll huff and I'll puff,
And I'll blow your house in.

PIG 1.   No, no. You can't come in.
Not by the hair of my chiny chin chin.

N.   So the wolf huffed, and he puffed, and he blew the house in and ate up the little pig.

The second little pig met a man with a bundle of sticks and said to him,

PIG 2.   Please, man, give me those sticks to build me a house.

N.   Which the man did, and the pig built a house with them. Soon along came the big bad wolf, who knocked on the door and said,

BBW.   Little pig, little pig.
Let me come in.
Or I'll huff and I'll puff,
And I'll blow your house in.

PIG 2.   No, no. You can't come in.
Not by the hair of my chiny chin chin.

Readers Theatre Staging of "The Three Little Pigs"

Pig 1 Pig 2 Pig 3

Narrator

Big Bad Wolf

Audience

N. So the wolf huffed, and he puffed, and he blew the house in and ate up the little pig.

The third little pig met a man with a load of bricks and said to him,

PIG 3. Please, man, give me those bricks to build me a house.

N. Which the man did and the pig built a house with them. Soon along came the big bad wolf, who knocked on the door and said,

BBW. Little pig, little pig,
Let me come in.
Or I'll huff and I'll puff,
And I'll blow your house in.

PIG 3.   No, no. You can't come in.
         Not by the hair of my chiny chin chin.

   N.   Well, the wolf huffed, and he puffed, and he huffed, and he puffed;
         but he could not blow the house in.

         Then the wolf was very angry and said he would come down the
         chimney to get the little pig.

         When the little pig heard that, he hung a pot full of water in the
         fireplace and built a blazing fire under it. The wolf came down the
         chimney and fell into the pot of boiling water. When he was fully
         cooked, the little pig ate him for supper and lived happily ever
         after.

Seasonal T-Scopes

Teacher-made tachistoscopes (or T-scopes) are effective devices for reinforcing
basic sight words. Children who are in the process of learning these frequently
used words need many exposures to them, and T-scopes provide a way for the
children to review them in a new format.

A T-scope is a device with an opening through which words (or phrases) are
shown in isolation. Words from the basic sight word list (see Appendix A) are
written on strips of poster board and pulled through the T-scope, revealing one
word at a time to be identified, on sight, by the reader.

For variety and interest, colorful T-scopes may be made to fit the season at
hand. If laminated they may be used year after year by different groups of students.

Purposes and Objectives

   1. To reinforce basic sight words
   2. To provide an independent word-study activity

Number of Participants

   One or two

Materials Needed

   □   Poster board in assorted colors and white
   □   Black felt-point pen

☐ Scissors

☐ Clear contact paper

Instructions for Making Aid

Cut colored poster board into holiday shapes and trim them with the black marker. Cut an opening in the middle. Glue a strip of poster board over the opening on the back to form a slot for the word strip as shown in the illustration. Make several word strips. Laminate each T-scope for durability.

Show students how to insert the word strip and how to pull it through, pronouncing each word as it appears in the opening. If two students work together, they may help each other with the words.

Variations and Teaching Hints

The following shapes make fine T-scopes: valentine hearts, Christmas packages, snowmen and women, shamrocks, Easter eggs, Jack-o'-lanterns, and ghosts.

Display and Storage

File T-scopes in folders with other holiday materials and use them only at the appropriate season.

Evaluation

1. Efficiency in use of basic sight words
2. Greater interest in independent word study

Seasonal T-scopes

Bleach Bottle Tachistoscope

For reinforcement of the most frequently used nouns, a T-scope is an enjoyable tool for primary students to use independently.

Any common noun that can be illustrated with a small picture is suitable for use in this acitivity (see Appendix B).

Purposes and Objectives

1. To practice recognizing on sight the most frequently used nouns
2. To recognize the noun as a naming word

Number of Participants

One to four

Materials Needed

☐ Empty plastic bleach bottle (two-quart size)
☐ Felt scraps
☐ All-purpose glue
☐ Corrugated cardboard
☐ Sharp knife
☐ Index cards (3" × 5")
☐ Used workbook for small pictures
☐ Felt-point pen

Instructions for Making Aid

1. Turn the bottle on its side with the handle up.
2. Cut a 2" × 4" opening toward the end of the bottle.
3. Use long brads to fasten a cardboard stand to the bottle to make it stationary.
4. With small scraps of felt and glue, add features to the bottle to make it look like an animal.
5. At the top of each index card, write a noun.
6. Near the bottom of each card, paste (or draw) a small picture to identify the noun.

Bleach Bottle Tachistoscope

Sample card for the bleach bottle tachistoscope

STUDENT DIRECTIONS

1. Place the cards in the bottle.

2. Read the first word.

3. Look in the spout to check the word.

4. If you are right, put the card on the table.

5. If you are wrong, put the card at the back of the deck.

6. Continue reading and checking until all cards are on the table.

Variations and Teaching Hints

Make up as many noun cards as time permits and divide them into decks of twenty each. Place them alongside the bleach bottle T-scope and give students the privilege of choosing the deck they will use.

A corresponding foreign word may be used along with the English one for students who are learning English as a second language.

Students may also be asked to use each noun in a sentence.

Display and Storage

The bleach bottle T-scope should be made available as part of the language center.

Evaluation

Look for an increase in sight vocabulary and for the ability to recognize nouns as naming words. Students may be tested by means of a quick-flash drill.

Sports Lingo

Tachistoscopic devices supplied with words found in the sports pages of the daily newspaper may be used with older students. The language of sports is rich in jargon—terminology that is fascinating to most children. Many sources may be used to collect the jargon, but the newspaper provides the most plentiful and consistent storehouse of words.

Students should divide themselves into teams based on their own enthusiasm for a sport and then begin mining the literature for words peculiar to the sport they have chosen. As wholesome competition develops among the teams, the word lists will grow longer and longer. This game is a painless method for getting students interested in newspapers, magazines, and other transient literature.

When the words are accumulated, they should be printed on strips of poster board to be used in the T-scopes that have been made in the shape of a familiar symbol for each sport. As students study and read with one another, they become familiar with pronunciation, meaning, and spelling. They also begin developing the habit of newspaper and magazine reading.

Purposes and Objectives

1. To reinforce the vocabulary of sports and athletics
2. To promote newspaper reading
3. To provide a means of independent word study

Number of Participants

Any number

Materials Needed

☐ Newspapers, magazines, paperbacks, brochures

☐ Poster board in assorted colors and white

☐ Black felt-point pens

☐ Scissors

Instructions for Making Aid

Cut colored poster board into the shapes of sports symbols and trim them with black markers. Cut an opening in the middle. Glue a strip of poster board over the opening on the back to form a slot for the word strip as shown in the illustration. Make as many T-scopes as there are sports represented.

STUDENT DIRECTIONS

1. Choose the sport you like best.

2. Join the group that will research your favorite sport.

3. Write down as many words as you can find that are used in your sport.

4. Print the words on strips of poster board.

5. Make a T-scope to represent your sport. The teacher will give you directions.

6. Study all the words collected by you and your classmates.

Variations and Teaching Hints

An excellent project for accelerated students is to have them research the origins of colorful words and phrases used in sports. Students may then share these curious stories with their classmates.

Display and Storage

The finished T-scopes should be placed in the classroom library center for several weeks, and students should be encouraged to add new words as they are encountered.

Evaluation

1. Evidence of a wider use and understanding of sports terminology
2. Greater interest in the daily newspaper and similar materials
3. Observable enthusiasm for independent word study
4. A greater number of sports terms appearing in the creative writing of students

Sports Lingo

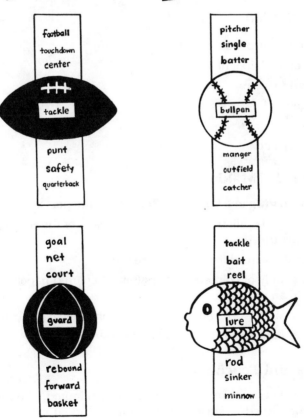

Sight Word Bingo

Acquiring a sight vocabulary is a major goal of beginning reading. The term *sight vocabulary* designates those words whose printed form and meaning are recognized instantly by the reader. Regardless of how a word is initially learned, sight words should be recognized immediately in various encounters with the printed form of that word. The Dolch list of 220 words is perhaps the best-known list of basic sight vocabulary (see Appendix A).

Purposes and Objectives

1. To reinforce understanding of basic sight words
2. To introduce new sight words

Number of Participants

Small group to entire class

Materials Needed

□ Cardboard or poster board
□ Small cards for sight words
□ Colored markers
□ Storage box
□ Envelopes
□ Cardboard box

Instructions for Making Aid

1. Make as many game boards as there are students (see illustration).
2. Write thirty-six different sight words on each of the Bingo game boards (see Appendix A).
3. Make each board different from the others.
4. Place a supply of colored markers (bits of colored paper, buttons, beans) in an envelope.
5. Write the sight words on cards of a uniform size (see illustration).
6. Keep the sight words in a small box for storage.

Variations and Teaching Hints

The ways to play classroom Bingo are almost unlimited. The version using sight words may be played in small groups (with a student caller) or with the entire class. The teacher could limit the time students have for identifying the words as one variation. Another alternative would be to use words from other lists—nouns, compounds, Wilson's Essential Vocabulary, and so forth.

STUDENT DIRECTIONS

1. Take one Bingo card and one envelope from the storage box.

2. Place the card and envelope on your desk.

3. As the teacher or caller says each word, place a marker on your Bingo card if you find the word on it.

4. The first person to complete a diagonal, vertical, or horizontal row on the card calls "Bingo."

5. The teacher or caller checks the card for accuracy.

SIGHT WORD BINGO

after	give	her	just	let	by
had	again	live	may	could	has
know	how	an	every	going	of
put	fly	open	any	some	take
from	them	stop	his	as	over
walk	when	him	once	then	ask

an

when

going

Storage

The game should be stored in an attractive box that includes the game boards, tokens, and call words. The Dolch words should be kept in a small box so they can be pulled easily by the caller.

Evaluation

1. Student interest in the game
2. Correct responses on the bingo card

Homophone Hunt

Primary children often have difficulty recognizing homophones—two words that are pronounced the same but have different spellings. Such words are particularly troublesome as children are learning to recognize words on sight. Regardless of how homophones are taught initially, students should be able to recognize their various uses. Interesting practice in using homophones is a means of increasing the basic sight vocabulary of a child.

Purposes and Objectives

1. To reinforce understanding of homophones
2. To introduce new homophones
3. To provide an independent word-study activity

Number of Participants

One or two

Materials Needed

☐ Poster board
☐ Felt-point marker
☐ Small basket
☐ Scissors
☐ List of homophones (see Appendix J)

Instructions for Making Aid

Cut fifteen egg-shaped ovals from poster board (see illustrations). Using the homophones found in Appendix J, print the words on each end of the egg. Cut the eggs between the words using a jagged line. Vary the jagged line between each pair of words so that only the correct pair will fit together when all the halves of the eggs are scattered. Make several sets of homophone eggs and store them in envelopes.

Students play Homophone Hunt by scattering the eggs faceup on a desk or table and matching the two halves. One child selects a homophone and tries to find a match. If the egg is successfully matched, the complete egg is placed in the basket and the next player takes a turn. Play continues until all the eggs are matched.

Variations and Teaching Hints

Several collections of homophone eggs should be developed to provide variation for the game. The eggs should contain easy homophones before introducing more difficult pairs. A similar game could be prepared using antonyms, synonyms, compound words, and so forth.

Storage

Homophone eggs might be stored in an egg-shaped hosiery container.

Evaluation

1. Improved recognition of homophones
2. Evidence of wider use of homophones

Compound Concentration

A compound word is composed of two independent words, each of which conveys a separate meaning. A compound word is one in which the meaning of the combined word is a blend of the other two words, as in "sandcastle" and "snowman." Children collect compound words they find in their reading, writing, and classroom experiences. Another way students come to better understand compound words is through games such as Concentration.

Purposes and Objectives

1. To understand that independent words may be combined to form new words
2. To provide practice in identifying compound words

Number of Participants

Two to four

Materials Needed

☐ Thirty-six index cards
☐ Black felt-point pen

Instructions for Making Aid

1. List eighteen compound words (see Appendix F)
2. Write each compound word on a separate card

Variations

A deck of forty-eight cards may be created after the students master the game. The game may be played by using synonyms, homonyms, antonyms, and so forth. Other interesting variations may be introduced by producing cards of varying levels of difficulty or with different point values.

Storage

Provide a case or box for the game. If more than one set of concentration cards is used, label and put a rubber band around them.

Evaluation

1. Completion of the game
2. Ability to identify compound words
3. Student self-evaluation

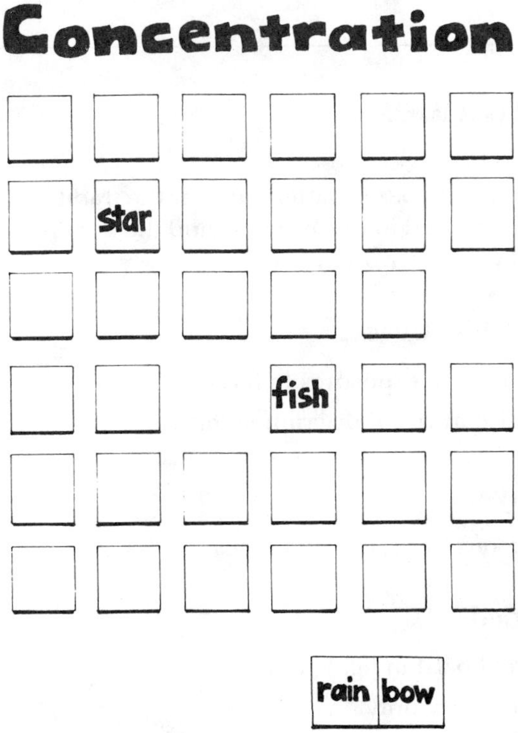
Concentration
star
fish
rain
bow

STUDENT DIRECTIONS

1. Shuffle the cards.

2. Place the cards facedown on a flat surface.

3. Select one player to start the game.

4. Turn two cards over and decide if the word is a compound.

5. If you make a match, keep the cards and take another turn.

6. If you do not make a match, turn the cards facedown.

7. The next player takes a turn.

8. The game is over when all cards are matched.

9. The winner is the player with the most pairs.

Word Dominoes

The game of Word Dominoes is patterned after the traditional game of dominoes except that words are used in place of dots and the dominoes are made of poster board rather than wood or ivory.

Purposes and Objectives

1. To provide multiple exposures to basic sight words
2. To give practice in visual discrimination

Number of Players

Two to four persons per set of dominoes

Materials Needed

☐ Six-ply poster board in light colors
☐ Paper cutter (heavy duty)
☐ Black felt-point pen

☐ Rubber bands

☐ Word lists (Appendix A)

Instructions for Making Aid

One set consists of twenty-eight dominoes. Seven words are repeated eight times in a set, each word being matched once with itself and once with every other word in the set.

A standard sheet of poster board, 22″ × 28″, makes forty-eight dominoes (see illustration). As a rule, the length of a domino should be twice its width. A heavy line drawn across the domino divides it in half.

In labeling a set of word dominoes, the teacher selects any seven words on which the student needs practice and assigns each word a numeral. The twenty-eight dominoes are then arranged in the pattern shown on pages 28–30. With a felt-point pen label each domino according to the diagrams. The illustration on page 30 is one example of a domino set made from the list of words given on the page. The diagram on page 30 shows the number pattern for placing words from any list of seven words.

STUDENT DIRECTIONS

1. Invite one, two, or three friends to play dominoes with you.

2. Find a good place to spread out the dominoes.

3. Shuffle (mix) the dominoes thoroughly.

4. Ask each player to choose five dominoes.

5. Leave extra dominoes facedown as a *bone pile* (draw pile).

6. Begin by placing a domino in the center of the playing area.

7. Pronounce each word that appears on the domino.

8. Ask the player on your left to place a domino with an identical word next to yours, as shown below.

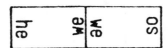

9. Ask the player to pronounce both the words on the domino played. Note: A player may ask for help with a word from any other player.

10. Continue taking turns to the left.

11. As play continues, the dominoes form a line. Corners may be made as needed to conform to the playing space. Players do not play on corners, but only on the ends of lines, as shown below.

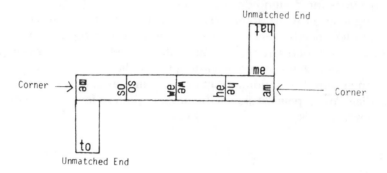

12. A player must draw a domino from the bone pile when no domino held will match or when all five dominoes in a hand have been used. A player must continue to draw until a matching word is drawn. Again, each word on the domino must be pronounced.

13. A *double* is a domino that has the same word on each end. The first double played in each game becomes a *spinner*. It is placed sideways in the line and has four playable sides, as shown below.

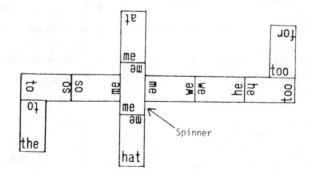

14. The first player to play all dominoes after the bone pile has been used up is the winner. The winner may play first in the next game.

Word Dominoes

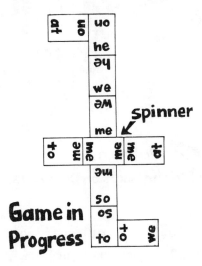

spinner

Game in
Progress

4½"

2¼"

Sample Card

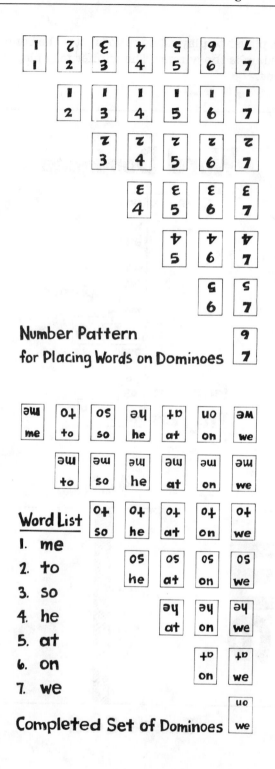

Number Pattern
for Placing Words on Dominoes

Word List

1. me
2. to
3. so
4. he
5. at
6. on
7. we

Completed Set of Dominoes

Variations and Teaching Hints

It is recommended that several sets of dominoes be made so that more than one group of students can play at the same time. Each set should contain a different group of words to provide a variety of practice. Word dominoes may be made more challenging to older students by using polysyllabic words and by requiring players to define the words or use them in sentences.

Storage

Each set of dominoes may be bound with a rubber band and stored together in a box labeled "Word Dominoes."

Evaluation

- ☐ Paper-and-pencil test using sight words
- ☐ Flash card test
- ☐ Teacher-made worksheets

Word Checkers

Another way to provide practice on basic sight words is a game played very much like the old-fashioned game of Checkers. The same red and black checkered board is used along with the checkers; however, in this activity, each player must read a word correctly in order to be able to move to a new square.

Purposes and Objectives

1. To reinforce basic sight words that have been introduced earlier
2. To provide an independent means of word study

Number of Participants

Two

Materials Needed

- ☐ Checkerboard
- ☐ Checkers
- ☐ Masking tape

☐   Black felt-point pen

☐   List of sight words (see Appendix A).

Instructions for Making Aid

With masking tape (on which words have been written) place two identical sight words on each of the red squares with one word right side up and the other upside down as shown in the illustration. The game is ready for playing. Demonstrate to students that the game is played in the following manner:

1. Choose red or black checkers and place them on the black squares.
2. Move or jump diagonally from one black square to another black square.
3. To move, a player must read correctly the word in front of the checker to be moved.
4. If the player is unable to read the word, he or she forfeits a turn; and the opponent may attempt to read the word.
5. Do not move backward or to a red square.
6. When a player jumps an opponent's checker, the man is captured and removed from the board.
7. A player cannot jump his or her own men.
8. Upon reaching the opponent's last row (the king's row), a player may crown a man by placing another checker on top of it making it a *king*. A king can move backward or forward.
9. The game ends when one player loses all checkers.
10. The winner is the player with checkers remaining.

Variations and Teaching Hints

Lift masking tape and change words frequently for reinforcement of additional words.

Storage

Store in game center for student selection.

Evaluation

1. Evidence of mastery of basic sight word list
2. Independence in studying words in a game format

Word Checkers

down		can		blue		and	
	is		help		go		find
not		make		little		it	
	said		red		play		one
we		up		two		the	
	run		our		funny		yellow
fast		did		do		in	
	cut		gave		big		away

Yes-No-Maybe Boxes

Students need to see their own progress and to have the satisfaction of knowing exactly what they have accomplished, especially in the area of reading. One way that you can illustrate progress to your students is to allow them to test themselves informally on basic sight words (see Appendix A).

The test is couched in a game format and the burden of proof rests on the child to decide how well he or she has mastered a particular sight word. The test itself is designed to reinforce the learning of frequently used words. To the child it becomes not only a testing device, but a learning game as well.

Purposes and Objectives

1. To help students ascertain how well basic sight words have been learned
2. To provide extra practice on the basic sight words

Number of Participants

One or two

Materials Needed

- ☐ Three cigar or shoe boxes or three one-pound coffee cans
- ☐ Assorted construction papers
- ☐ Cellophane tape
- ☐ Scissors
- ☐ Black felt-point pen
- ☐ Set of cards containing Dolch words (see Appendix A)
- ☐ Set of cards containing high-frequency nouns (see Appendix B)

Instructions for Making Aid

Cover the boxes with colored construction paper. Place a face with features on each box. Label boxes "yes," "no," and "maybe." Place cards in packs beside the boxes.

STUDENT DIRECTIONS

1. Select a pack of word cards.

2. Look at the first word.

3. If you know the word, put it in the "yes" box. If you have to think about the word, put it in the "maybe" box. If you do not know the word, put it in the "no" box.

4. Count the "yes" words.

5. Take the test again later.

Variations and Teaching Hints

When two students work together on this activity, they are able to help each other. As children read books and other materials, they gain a knowledge of sight words. Eventually all the words will belong in the "yes" box. Once students have learned all the words on sight, the game may become a spelling activity in which one child spells the word to another.

Storage

Store in game center to be used as needed.

Evaluation

1. Increase in the number of sight words mastered
2. Awareness that some words are used much more frequently than others
3. Improvement in oral reading as sight words are mastered

Sight Word Sorting Boxes

The Magic Key

Sequence, an important element of reading comprehension, refers to the order in which ideas or events are presented. For example, which event did the author convey at the beginning, middle, and end of a story? Sequential organization is usually classified into one of three patterns: (1) chronological (first, second, third), (2) spatial or descriptive (from area to area or location to location), and (3) expository or conceptual (general to specific, cause to effect, question to answer). Students use such patterns regularly in their lives and encounter them frequently in their reading.

Purposes and Objectives

1. To reinforce the concept of language sequence
2. To give practice in literal and inferential comprehension
3. To teach the concept that ideas and events occur in a logical sequence

Number of Participants

One

Materials Needed

- □ Spirit (ditto) masters box or similar container
- □ Cardboard or poster board
- □ Pictures and/or text from a library book
- □ Water-based markers
- □ Glue
- □ String
- □ Large nail
- □ Scissors
- □ Construction paper or plastic covering
- □ Clear contact paper

Instructions for Making Aid

1. Cut the box as shown in the illustration.
2. Punch three (or more) holes in the box as illustrated.
3. Decorate the box appropriately with construction paper, plastic, and so forth.

4. Cut five (or more) cardboard pieces, as shown in the illustration, so that they fit into the box.

5. Cut the bottom of the cardboard (as shown in the pattern). The cutout portion becomes the correct answer. Vary the position of the correct answer.

6. Mount the picture, the reading material, and the question, on the cardboard.

7. Attach a large nail to the box with a piece of string.

8. Make several sets of questions.

STUDENT DIRECTIONS

1. Study the picture or event described on the card.

2. Think about the story. Did the event happen at the beginning? Near the middle? At the end of the story?

3. Place the key in the correct hole where the incident happened.

4. Try to remove the card. If you can remove the card, your answer is correct. If you cannot remove the card, your answer is wrong. Try again.

5. When you come to the first card, you have finished the set.

6. Return materials to the storage box.

Variations and Teaching Hints

This activity may be adapted to a wide variety of problems requiring a single answer. The questions could be modified to *multiple-choice* or *true-false* formats. If you have students who are learning English, this activity may be adapted by giving the clues in a foreign language. For evaluation purposes, the teacher might create a student record sheet so that the number of correct answers may be recorded.

Display and Storage

Store the card packs and magic key inside a display box so that students can select their own activity.

Evaluation

1. Success in determining the correct answers
2. Interest in the activity
3. Ability to identify an idea or event in the proper sequence

The Magic Key

Game Box

Sample Card

On each card, cut 3 squares that align with holes on box front. In position of "correct" answer, cut away the card bottom to form a slot.

The Question Box

It is imperative for young readers to develop the habit of looking for the answers to six questions—Who? What? When? Where? Why? How?—if they are to fully comprehend newspaper and magazine articles. This activity is designed to help students acquire a tool they will find useful throughout life.

Purposes and Objectives

1. To improve reading comprehension
2. To encourage students to read and remember details in newspaper and magazine articles

Number of Participants

Six

Materials Needed

- ☐ Shoe box
- ☐ White poster board
- ☐ Six ball-point pens in different colors
- ☐ Scissors
- ☐ Mat knife
- ☐ Paste
- ☐ Six newspaper articles

Instructions for Making Aid

Cover the shoe box with paper as though wrapping a gift. Cut six slots in the top. Decorate the box with question marks.

Make six word cards according to the directions in the illustration. Label them "Who?" "What?" "When?" "Where?" "Why?" and "How?" Place the cards inside the slots so that the words disappear from sight.

Variations and Teaching Hints

Choose a wide variety of interesting articles ranging from easy-to-read to difficult. Some may be collected from children's magazines.

Allow ample time for students to read thoughtfully and carefully. Check their work for accuracy. A great deal of reading practice will take place during each relay.

STUDENT DIRECTIONS

1. Choose five friends to work with you.

2. Sit in a circle or around a table.

3. Give each person a colored pen.

4. Give each person a newspaper article.

5. Ask each person to draw a word card from the question box.

6. Find the answer to your question in the article and underline it.

7. Pass the article to the next person, who answers another question.

8. When all six answers have been marked in different colors, put the articles on the bulletin board for others to read.

The Question Box

tag ⇨

⇦ tag

Slots for <u>who</u>, <u>what</u>, <u>when</u>, <u>where</u>, <u>how</u>, and <u>why</u> tags.

when

Evaluation

1. Increased interest in newspapers and magazines
2. Improved reading comprehension
3. Greater accuracy in recalling details

Newspaper Art

An art-newspaper activity is an excellent means of helping young readers to interpret what they read with greater accuracy. The students simply select an interesting article from the newspaper and then depict it in art form, adding as many details as possible. When the paintings are finished, and the articles added, they are posted at eye level for others to read.

Purposes and Objectives

1. To encourage reading of the newspaper
2. To improve interpretive reading skills
3. To provide a creative art experience

Number of Participants

Any number

Materials Needed

- Newspapers
- Crayons, colored chalk, watercolors, tempera paint, and colored felt-point pens
- Large, white art paper
- Assorted construction papers
- Scissors
- Paste

Instructions for Making Aid

Ask students to scan the newspapers for an interesting article that might be interpreted in art. When an article is selected, the student rereads it carefully and then paints a picture that tells the same story. Both the article and the painting are mounted on a large piece of colored construction paper.

STUDENT DIRECTIONS

1. Look through the newspaper and select an article that you find interesting.

2. Cut the article from the paper.

3. Read the article once again and paint a picture of the story.

4. Paste the article on your picture.

5. Put your art work on the bulletin board.

6. Read all the articles selected by your friends.

Newspaper Art

Variations and Teaching Hints

When the pictures are removed from the bulletin board, they may be preserved in a large scrapbook and placed in the library center for future reading.

Evaluation

1. Evidence of improved ability to interpret reading materials
2. Greater attention to details in reading
3. Increased efficiency in reading the daily newspaper

Four-Fold Quiz

Reading comprehension improves when students learn to look for the *six honest serving men* of writing—Who?, What?, Where?, When?, Why?, and How? One way to help children develop the habit of reading with these essential questions in mind is to have students discover answers in newspaper articles.

Purposes and Objectives

1. To help students read with better comprehension
2. To help students remember more of the factual information they read
3. To improve expository writing

Number of Participants

Any number

Materials Needed

☐ Art paper
☐ Felt-point pens
☐ Newspapers
☐ Scissors
☐ Paste

Instructions for Making Aid

Cut several squares of art paper approximately 8 ½″ × 8 ½″. Ask students to fold each corner of a square into the middle as shown in the illustration. Have them use felt pens to write "How?" and "Why?" in the middle and "Who?", "What?", "Where?", and "When?" on the four flaps as shown. The students now select a newspaper article for analysis. As they find each answer, they write it in the appropriate space on the inside of the folded paper.

To display the finished work, students should cut out the article they chose and paste it on one end of a page of colored construction paper. On the other end they should paste the folded paper containing their writing. The folded paper should be pasted so that the flaps can still be lifted for reading.

STUDENT DIRECTIONS

1. Fold the four corners of your square into the middle.

2. Write "Why?" and "How?" in the center.

3. Write "Who?", "What?", "When?", and "Where?" on the flaps.

4. Read a newspaper article and write the answers on the folded paper.

5. Put the article and your writing on the bulletin board for others to read.

Four-Fold Quiz

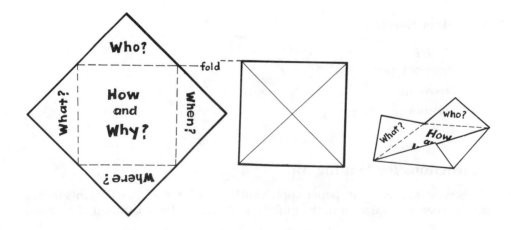

Variations and Teaching Hints

You can help students transfer, to their own writing, their understanding of the key factors found in reading material by having them consciously answer each question in essays and reports.

Evaluation

1. Observable improvement in reading comprehension
2. Evidence of writing that is well organized and thorough

Trademark Montage

Some of the first and best reading materials for young children are the words and phrases they find all around them everyday. Well before they enter school, most children note billboard words, traffic signs, candy wrappers, their own names on Christmas gifts, and a great array of advertisements in newspapers and magazines.

On entering school students find still more of these *life-coping* words—names over coat hooks, the day's schedule on the chalkboard, the lunch menu on the bulletin board, and countless signs and labels needed for classroom living.

For helping students further develop the habit of reading words in the everyday environment, a montage of trademarks, brand names, and logos is very effective. "Montage" comes from the French word "monter," which is a composite picture made by combining several photographs to create a new image.

In the primary classroom, students create montages by cutting pictures (or in this case labels) from magazines or newspapers and pasting them together on a surface with their edges slightly overlapping. The finished montages will suggest the verbal world of advertising.

Purposes and Objectives

1. To stimulate an interest in trademarks, labels, and logos
2. To encourage an awareness of reading in the environment
3. To give practice in selecting, classifying, cutting, and pasting

Number of Participants

Any number

Materials Needed

- ☐ Discarded magazines
- ☐ Poster board
- ☐ Wheat paste (wallpaper paste)
- ☐ Brushes
- ☐ Scissors

Trademark Montage

Instructions for Making Aid

Lead a discussion on trademarks in advertising and show familiar examples.

Ask students to cut words they recognize from magazines and paste them on the poster board. Mount the finished montages on the bulletin board for rereading.

Variations and Teaching Hints

Allow students to make as many of the montage posters as time permits. Both individual and group projects are enjoyable and beneficial. Montages might be created using classifications such as the following:

Automobiles

Toothpastes

Soft drinks

Candy

Canned vegetables and fruits

Restaurants

Grocery stores

Evaluation

1. Interest in trademarks and brand names
2. Increased skill in classifying
3. Awareness of reading in the environment

Propaganda Detective

An important factor in developing objectivity along with reading comprehension is the ability to detect propaganda in literature and to recognize the type of propaganda that is being employed to mold the reader's opinion. To acquaint students with the main propaganda devices, you can use newspaper and magazine advertisements as convenient sources of illustrations. Suitable ads should be collected, discussed, labeled as to type, and mounted on the bulletin board for further study.

Purposes and Objectives

1. To provide an accurate definition of "propaganda"
2. To teach the ten most common propaganda devices
3. To help students become more objective and discriminating in reading and listening

Number of Participants

Any number

Materials Needed

☐ Magazines and newspapers

☐ Scissors

☐ Wheat paste

☐ Assorted construction papers

☐ Black felt-point pen

☐ Chart of propaganda types

Instructions for Making Aid

Discuss with students the different propaganda techniques used in radio, television, billboard, magazine, and newspaper advertising. The following list describes the types encountered most frequently.

TYPES OF PROPAGANDA

"Propaganda" is a methodical plan for spreading ideas or opinions to promote a cause or product.

1. Bandwagon advertising. Suggests that everyone else is enjoying this product; you should too. Usually employs large crowds of people in a *bandwagon* effect.
2. Testimonial or personal endorsement. Employs very well-known athletes, movie stars, and public figures endorsing products. Implies that if you use the product you will be as successful and popular as they are.
3. Repetition, hypnotism. Uses a slogan repeated over and over to mesmerize the listener or reader. Also seeks to have the consumer commit the slogan to memory.

4. Plain folks or down-home advertising. Employs ordinary people who are neighborly and folksy to promote products. Implies that an ordinary person is honest and would not cheat or deceive you.

5. Ego building, snob appeal. Suggests that if you use a certain product, you too may belong to this exclusive group. Implies that you are superior and should have an advantage over others.

6. Propaganda using emotional words, patriotic slogans. Employs words such as "mother," "grandmother," "church," "U.S.A." Suggests that if you are a good mother, Christian, citizen, or whatever, you will use this product.

7. Advertising promoting value, durability. Emphasizes the idea of *more for less*. Promises that a product will last longer and save the consumer more money than competing products.

8. Straw-man advertising. Creates a problem where none exists in order to sell a product. "If you have trouble sleeping at night, use this product."

9. Sex appeal. Features beautiful women and handsome men promoting products. Suggests that if you use this product you will be attractive to the opposite sex.

10. Card stacking. States all the claims (stacks the cards) in favor of one product.

STUDENT DIRECTIONS

1. Find advertisements that show propaganda.

2. Decide what type is being used.

3. Check with a friend to find whether or not he or she agrees.

4. Cut out the ad.

5. Paste it on colored paper.

6. Label it according to propaganda type.

7. Place the ad on the bulletin board.

When the students are familiar with the various methods used to influence readers and listeners, and have verbally presented several examples, ask them to cut graphic examples from newspapers and magazines. Students can then mount them on colored construction paper and tack them on a "Propaganda" bulletin board.

Variations and Teaching Hints

Conduct this activity as a mini-unit and plan for it to continue a week or longer. Allow students ample time to discuss each propaganda type and be prepared for differences of opinion regarding ads and commercials. An excellent resource for the teacher is *The Hidden Persuaders* by Vance Packard. (New York: David McKay Co., 1957.)

Evaluation

1. Evidence of a healthy skepticism toward advertising
2. An increased ability to read critically

Propaganda Detective

Browse Boxes

Consumer materials of all kinds make for interesting reading in a student's spare time. Not only are such "found" materials fascinating to read, but they also offer excellent practice in literal comprehension skills.

Functional kits made up of everyday reading matter are suitable for all grades and ability levels. The kits may be composed simply of pictures, labels, and logos or upgraded to include catalogs, brochures, and employment application blanks. Browse boxes are individualized because they are developed with a particular student, or group of students, in mind.

The use of browse boxes should be nonstructured and informal, with students choosing when they will go to them and which pieces they will take out for reading. Students may choose to read an entire piece of material or only a portion of it.

Because students are given plenty of freedom in using the consumer kits, they may see them as quite different from most other school assignments and therefore more appealing. The value of this activity will be greatly diminished if too many rules and guidelines are imposed.

Purposes and Objectives

1. To help develop the habit of reading printed material wherever it is encountered in the environment
2. To help develop the habit of reading carefully for facts and information
3. To encourage the reading of directions on consumer products

Number of Participants

Any number

Materials Needed

Any kind of consumer material that will be of interest to your students is suitable for browse boxes. The following list shows some of the possibilities:

- ☐ Newspapers
- ☐ Driver manual
- ☐ Maps
- ☐ Phone books
- ☐ Scout manuals
- ☐ Menus, recipes

- ☐ Magazines
- ☐ Comic strips
- ☐ Travel folders
- ☐ Calendars
- ☐ First aid manuals
- ☐ Cookbooks

- ☐ Pattern books
- ☐ Trading stamp books
- ☐ Tax forms
- ☐ Crossword puzzles
- ☐ Scripts of plays
- ☐ Career booklets
- ☐ Health, safety booklets
- ☐ Mail order catalogs
- ☐ Application blanks
- ☐ Song texts
- ☐ Labels, boxtops
- ☐ T.V. guides
- ☐ "How-to-do-it" directions
- ☐ Grooming booklets

Instructions for Making Aid

Cover two or three small sturdy boxes with colored wrapping paper and label each with stick-on letters. Laminate the boxes with clear contact paper. Fill each box with the consumer materials that you and your students have collected. Leave space for new additions such as weekly T.V. guides. To avoid congestion, place the kits in various parts of the classroom.

Variations and Teaching Hints

A multicultural awareness may be enhanced by the addition of menus, recipes, directions, labels and other materials printed in languages other than English.

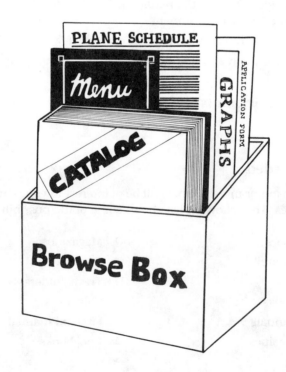

> ### STUDENT DIRECTIONS
>
> 1. In your free time, thumb through a Browse Box.
>
> 2. Select several pieces that you would like to read.
>
> 3. Take the pieces to your desk.
>
> 4. Return the pieces for others to read.

Storage

Store materials as shown in the following figure.

Evaluation

1. Evidence of greater interest in consumer reading
2. Improved skill in reading factual information
3. Greater awareness of everyday reading in the environment
4. A willingness to read directions on consumer products

Alligator Bog Map Skills

Pictures, charts, graphs, tables, and maps can provide a wealth of information for students. Graphic materials, however, are not always interpreted correctly by children; nor are they always well utilized. Filling in an outline map focuses attention on details but does not promote an understanding of map symbols. Development of the ability to read maps and other graphic information should proceed from the relatively simple to the more complex. Students can become acquainted with basic map symbols and their meanings by playing a version of the familiar game Old Maid.

Purposes and Objectives

1. To identify common map symbols
2. To strengthen and reinforce the usage of map symbols

Number of Participants

Two to six

Materials Needed

☐   Deck of blank playing cards

☐   Map symbols

☐   Water-based marker

Instructions for Making Aid

1. Obtain a deck of blank playing cards.

2. Use a deck of forty-five cards for playing Alligator Bog.

3. On one of the cards, draw or glue an Alligator Bog similar to the illustration. This card is similar to the Old Maid card.

4. Draw or glue twenty-two familiar map symbols on one-half of the cards and their corresponding titles on the other half.

5. Store the complete deck in a container.

Variations and Teaching Hints

Several different sets of cards should be prepared to add variety to the game and introduce more map symbols. Students may then select the deck they wish to use when more than one game has been prepared.

STUDENT DIRECTIONS

1. Shuffle the cards and deal them, one at a time, facedown to all of the players.

2. You might receive one more card than some of the other players but this does not matter.

3. You should be careful not to let any of the other players see the cards you hold.

4. Look at the cards, and match as many pairs as possible. Place all matched pairs faceup on the table.

5. The dealer begins play by drawing one card from the hand of the player to the left.

6. If the drawn card matches one in your hand, place the matched pair on the table. If not, keep the card and add it to your hand.

7. Your turn ends and the player to your left draws one card from your hand, and so on.

8. The game continues until all pairs of cards are matched and one player is left holding the Alligator Bog. That player is the loser.

Storage

Store card packs in a box labeled "Alligator Bog."

Evaluation

1. Evidence of improved ability to interpret map symbols
2. Greater attention to visual symbols
3. Interest in playing the game

Alligator Bog Map Skills

Marsh

US Highway

Sample "Old Maid" Card ➡

(This is the only single in the deck. All others are pairs.)

Alligator Bog

US Highway

Interstate

Ranch or Farm Road

Multilane Highway

Interchange

Rest Area

Toll Barrier

Service Area

Paved Road

Unpaved Road

Overpass

Underpass

Ferry

Trail

Railroad

★ State Capital

County Seat

City

Town

Buildings

School

Church

Cemetery

Quarry

Mineshaft

Stream

Intermittent Stream

Lake

Falls

Rapids

Well

Well with Spring

Dam

State Park

Campsite

Picnic Area

Winter Sports Area

Fishery

Wildlife Area

Commercial Airport

Military Airport

Local Airfield

Marsh

Desert

Road Map Reading

We live in a world where charts, diagrams, and maps are used extensively, but all too often students seem baffled by symbolic and graphic information. Many students do not fully understand the abstraction of a map or chart, and they need specific instruction from the teacher. It is often necessary for the language arts teacher to review with students the legend of a map, the specifics of symbols used on a chart, and other aspects of processing visual information before conducting a study of this kind of material.

Purposes and Objectives

1. To help students recognize symbolic information found on maps
2. To make use of various types of maps to locate specific information
3. To develop an understanding of map vocabulary and symbols

Number of Participants

One to six

Materials Needed

- ☐ City maps
- ☐ State road maps
- ☐ United States map
- ☐ Maps of other countries
- ☐ World maps
- ☐ Oaktag or cardboard
- ☐ Large envelopes
- ☐ Water-based markers
- ☐ Clear contact paper

Instructions for Making Aid

1. Gather a variety of different types of maps.
2. Cut the maps into six to nine pieces of equal size.
3. Glue the map sections to pieces of cardboard.
4. Laminate the map pieces with clear contact paper for added durability.

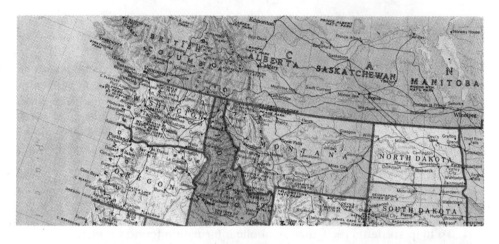

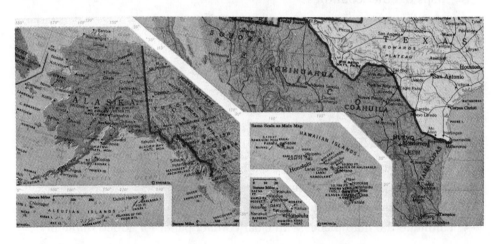

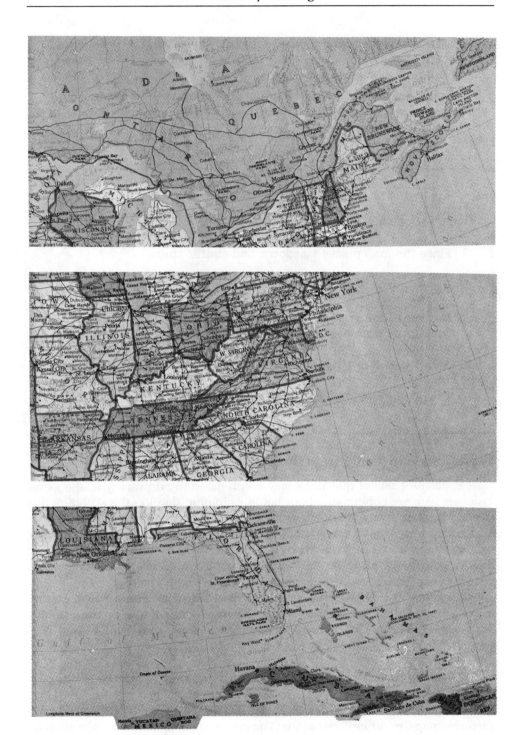

5. Create a road map quiz similar to the one illustrated. The questions should be general and applicable to all of the maps. Note: Not every answer will appear on every map.

6. Give the students a specific length of time to repsond to the questions on an answer sheet or by marking directly on the map with a water-based marker or wax crayon.

STUDENT DIRECTIONS

1. Select one of the envelopes from the file.

2. Place the map pieces facedown and shuffle them.

3. Draw a piece from the pile.

4. Answer as many of the questions from the card as you can during the time period given.

5. Give yourself one point for each correct answer.

6. The player with the most points is the winner.

Variations and Teaching Hints

Several different sets of questions may be prepared to add variety to the game. Teachers who are concerned about helping children develop the skill of noting directions could also ask students to place directional information directly on a map with a water-based marker. For increased awareness about other cultures, map questions could be followed by a discussion about different countries and their languages. For example, the historical origin of a specific location could be traced, foreign words could be analyzed, or folklore could be read.

Other types of maps—aerial maps, railroad maps, air route maps, county maps, school district maps, and topography maps—might also be used to play Road Map Reading. This activity is related to Name That Symbol and Alligator Bog.

Storage

Store maps and questions in a legal-size envelope. It may be decorated with pictures, maps, or other illustrations. The entire set should then be placed in an attractive storage box and labeled "Road Map Reading."

Evaluation

1. Ability to recognize and locate various map symbols
2. Interest in playing the game
3. Awareness of foreign languages, lands, and cultures

ROAD MAP READING

1. Find a state capital.
2. Find an interstate highway.
3. Find a national park.
4. Find a north-south river.
5. Find an island.
6. Find an airport.
7. Find a college or university.
8. Find a military base.
9. Find a mountain range.
10. Find a marshland.
11. Find a national monument.
12. Find a lake.
13. Find an Indian reservation.
14. Find a canal.
15. Find a city that is also the name of a president.

PART II

ACTIVITIES TO ENRICH WRITING

Chinese Tangrams

A fascinating puzzle called a *tangram* involves fitting a square, a parallelogram, and five triangles together to form various patterns. Many tangram puzzles are carved from ivory or wood, but less expensive ones can be made from squares of sturdy cardboard.

Books of tangram patterns are available in hobby shops, but children benefit from creating their own designs. When a pleasing design is made, the child may write or tell a story about it.

Purposes and Objectives

1. To study an ancient hobby
2. To create an interesting writing assignment
3. To provide an opportunity for oral language practice

Number of Participants

One or two per puzzle

Materials Needed

- ☐ Several pieces of sturdy, colored mat board
- ☐ Heavy-duty paper cutter
- ☐ Small brown envelopes for storage

Instructions for Making Aid

Follow the pattern on page 65 to cut the cardboard into tangram puzzles. Use a different color for each puzzle in case pieces become mixed inadvertently.

Place each tangram puzzle in a brown envelope. The puzzles are now ready for student use. When introducing tangrams to children, the teacher should demonstrate how to make several designs.

Students often become completely captivated by the puzzles and ask to work with them day after day. Originally developed in China, tangram puzzles have been a popular hobby for more than three-hundred years in the Western world. It is said that Napoleon Bonaparte, John Quincy Adams, Lewis Carroll, and Edgar Allan Poe puzzled for hours over tangrams. These puzzles were often called *head breakers*.

STUDENT DIRECTIONS

1. Take a tangram from the envelope and place the pieces on your desk.

2. Arrange the pieces to form a plant, animal, person, or other shape.

3. Show your design to a friend and describe it.

4. Write a story about your favorite tangram design.

Variations and Teaching Hints

Make a study of the ancient art of creating tangram designs. An excellent resource to use with elementary students is *The Eighth Book of Tan: 700 Tangrams* by Sam Loyd (New York: Dover, 1968).

Use tangrams as an introduction to paper folding, string games, and other geometrical puzzles.

Because cardboard tangrams are very inexpensive and easily replaced, a student who creates an unusually effective design should be encouraged to glue it onto paper and preserve it.

Storage

Store puzzles in manila envlopes and place in game center.

Evaluation

1. Development of independence in working on a tedious mental task
2. Evidence of lasting interest in solving puzzles of various types
3. Interest in writing a descriptive essay

Pattern for the Chinese Tangram

Several Tangram Designs

Writing Trifolders

To be able to write effectively, students need (1) something to write about, (2) a reason for writing, (3) help with word acquisition and spelling, and (4) a way to make good use of the finished product. Writing trifolders provides all four ingredients.

The left side of the folder contains general rules for writing a letter, short story, essay, poem, or other form of composition. The middle panel contains a picture or a model to stimulate writing. The right side contains a list of words likely to be needed in the writing.

Because creative writing is a rather private and lonely task, the completed folder is shaped so that it can stand in front of the writer to form a small study carrel.

Purposes and Objectives

1. To stimulate ideas for creative writing topics
2. To provide a guide or model for writing
3. To enrich the spelling vocabulary
4. To improve punctuation and capitalization skills

Number of Participants

One per folder

Materials Needed

- Manila folders
- Pictures, art prints, greeting cards, and other illustrations
- Scissors
- Black felt-point pen
- Masking tape
- Paste

Instructions for Making Aid

Cut manila folders along the fold line. Tape three equal parts together to form a three-sided folder. Three manila folders are required to make two trifolders.

Paste an illustration on the center panel of the folder. On the left panel, print directions for writing about the picture, listing skills to be emphasized. Directions might include punctuation and capitalization reminders, questions to be answered about the picture, and so forth. On the right panel, print a list of appropriate words from which the student may draw while writing about the picture.

When the writing is finished and has been proofread (see proofreading marks, p. 000) the student may paste it in a large scrapbook made of wrapping paper. Once the book is filled with stories, it should be placed in the library center.

STUDENT DIRECTIONS

1. Select a folder you like.

2. Study the picture.

3. Read the directions.

4. Write about the picture.

5. If you wish, use some of the spelling words on the folder.

6. Ask the teacher to proofread your work.

7. Correct your writing.

8 Create an illustration for your writing.

9. Paste your writing in the scrapbook.

10. Invite your friends to read your writing.

Variations and Teaching Hints

Make as many folders as time permits to give students a good selection. Supply words in foreign languages as well as in English for bilingual students.

Storage

Store folders in a file drawer and label each folder with a small picture or phrase to aid in selection

Evaluation

1. Improvement in writing skills
2. Enlarged spelling vocabulary
3. Improvement in use of punctuation and capitalization

Story Writing Folders

Shape Books

Books made in the shape of interesting and familiar objects are an effective way to stimulate the writing of short stories. Young children who are just learning to express themselves in writing enjoy a group project of this type in which they cooperate to write a one-of-a-kind book.

Purposes and Objectives

1. To provide motivation for creative writing
2. To assist primary children in developing writing skills
3. To produce interesting reading material

Number of Participants

Any number

Materials Needed

- ☐ Lined paper
- ☐ Lightweight poster board in several colors
- ☐ Scissors
- ☐ Black felt-point pen
- ☐ Paper fasteners (brads)

Instructions for Making Aid

Draw shapes, similar to those in the illustration, on the colored poster board. Add features with a black marker. Cut out the shapes. Cut ten to twenty pages of notebook paper in the same shape. Lines on the paper should run horizontally because students will be writing on them. Use a paper brad to fasten the notebook pages between the covers.

When the books are ready for students to use, they write their own imaginative stories focusing on the shape of the book. Allot two sides of one page for each student and remind them to sign their names to their own pages. As the booklets circulate in the class, they become filled with creative stories. The books should be placed in the library center for all to enjoy.

STUDENT DIRECTIONS

1. Select a shape book that you like.

2. Write a story in it.

3. Write about the shape.

4. Ask a friend to proofread your writing.

5. Sign your story.

Variations and Teaching Hints

Books may be designed in keeping with the holidays, and shapes such as a Christmas tree, stocking, gift package, snowman and woman, valentine, shamrock, flower, umbrella, Jack-o'-lantern, ghost, witch, or turkey can be used. Hobbies, collections, and sports are also suitable subjects for shape books.

Storage

Books in progress are stored in the writing center and completed ones in the library center.

Evaluation

1. Increased interest in the creative writing of short stories
2. Interest in reading the student-made books

Shape Books

Collection Compositions

Students in middle elementary school are serious collectors. They collect baseball cards, beer cans, old bottles, matchbooks, bubblegum cards, "hot wheels" cars, dolls, doll furniture, and almost anything else imaginable. Children's collections are extremely important to them; and the intensity with which they sort, classify, and arrange the items is a complete mystery to most adults. Such devotion to a hobby provides a natural subject for research, creative writing, and oral reporting. No motivating buildup is needed for this project.

Many children who collect objects have no idea that there are printed materials about their collections or at least, similar types of collections. It is almost as much a surprise for them to discover literature about their hobbies as it is to find a teacher who is interested in them.

Purposes and Objectives

1. To provide a relevant topic for expository writing
2. To create enthusiasm for library research
3. To create interesting subjects for oral reports

Number of Participants

Any number

Materials Needed

☐ Poster board
☐ Stick-on letters
☐ Picture of a collection
☐ List of your library's books related to hobbies and collections

Instructions for Making Aid

Make an attractive, colorful poster containing an illustration and a caption that reads "Collection Compositions." Display the poster in a prominent place in the classroom and use it as a focal point in a lively discussion on collecting and collections.

When sufficient interest has been generated, make arrangements for students to research, take notes, and write a report on their own collections. To highlight the activity, students should be permitted to bring in samples of their collections and to make brief, informal, oral reports.

Variations and Teaching Hints

After you have corrected the collection compositions and returned them to the students for recopying, the reports may be mounted in a class scrapbook and illustrated with student art work.

Evaluation

1. A polished piece of informative writing from each student
2. Effective library research based on a topic of personal interest
3. An oral report that is enjoyable to hear

STUDENT DIRECTIONS

1. Do you have a collection?

2. Look in the library and find information on your collection.

3. Take notes for a report on it.

4. Write a composition about your collection.

5. Plan to bring part of your collection to school at a scheduled time.

6. Prepare a short oral report for the class.

Picture Postcards

Students often write letters and postcards that are very interesting. When children know that what they write is actually to be mailed to someone, they are more likely to be concerned about accuracy. To create special interest in the project, have them first make artistic picture postcards "suitable for framing."

Purposes and Objectives

1. To improve the quality of personal letter writing
2. To provide a creative art experience

Number of Participants

Any number

Materials Needed

- ☐ Thin white poster board
- ☐ Crayons in assorted colors
- ☐ Black tempera paint
- ☐ One-inch soft brush
- ☐ Scissors
- ☐ Clear contact paper
- ☐ Paper cutter

Instructions for Making Aid

Using a paper cutter, cut the poster board into postcard-size rectangles approximately 4" × 6". Have students sketch pictures of their own creation on the cards. Landscapes, seascapes, or flower pictures are all suitable subjects. Show the students how to color their pictures heavily with wax crayons. Use a thin, black tempera wash over the crayon to form a batik effect as the wax resists the liquid paint. Cover each picture with clear contact paper to deepen the batik look and also to prevent cracking in the mail.

Variations and Teaching Hints

This is an excellent activity for all students at the upper elementary level; but it is especially good for accelerated students as an ongoing, spare-time activity. Keep needed materials available and ask students to provide their own stamps.

Notes may first be written and corrected on a separate sheet of paper before being copied onto the cards.

Evaluation

1. Increased interest in letter writing
2. Improved skills in personal letter writing

Picture Postcards

FRONT

BACK

Dear Uncle Bill,
I made this card for you by myself. I hope you like it. I do.
Love, Robin

STAMP

Name _____

Address _____

_____

_____

STUDENT DIRECTIONS

1. Draw a picture on each of your cards.

2. Color it heavily with crayons.

3. Paint over your crayon picture with black paint.

4. When your picture is dry, cover it with a piece of clear contact paper.

5. Address the back of your card to a friend or relative.

6. Write a note to your friend or relative.

7. Put a stamp on your card and mail it.

8. Make more cards if you have time.

Mask Makers

Down through the ages, people in all parts of the world have worn masks to disguise themselves and to transform and protect themselves. Students in the elementary classroom usually make and wear masks to entertain themselves and others, yet they also can appreciate the fact that some people wore masks for very serious occasions, such as healing and burial rituals.

There is probably no activity that provides more opportunities for cultural understanding than a unit on mask making in which students not only create masks but also research and write about them. Small groups may be formed to study the masks of Africa, Japan, and Greece. Other groups may elect to read and write about masks worn by the American Indians, the Eskimos of Alaska, or the Polynesian people of the South Pacific.

Masks of all types may be made from papier-mâché applied over an inflated balloon. Students should choose partners who want to create shapes similar to theirs, because after the balloon is covered with several thicknesses of paper strips and allowed to dry, it may be cut in half with scissors to form bases for two masks.

Purposes and Objectives

1. To provide incentive for research and creative writing

2. To promote cultural awareness and understanding

3. To give students a creative art experience

Number of Participants

Any number

Materials Needed

☐ Newspapers

☐ Wheat paste

☐ Round balloons

☐ Tempera paint

☐ Collection of scraps such as felt, paper, yarn, buttons, and beads (for trim)

☐ Shellac

☐ Dowel or broomstick for displaying masks

STUDENT DIRECTIONS

1. Read about masks in encyclopedias and reference books.

2. Decide on a country you wish to represent with your mask.

3. Make a papier-mâché mask according to the teacher's instructions.

4. Write a factual story, based on research, about your mask.

5. Paste your report in the mask scrapbook.

Instructions for Making Aid

Insert an inflated balloon part way into a large milk carton and tape it to the carton to form a stand as shown in the illustration. Dip strips of newspaper into paste that has been mixed to the consistency of thick cream. Apply wet strips to the balloon until it is covered with at least four layers. Allow the base to dry thoroughly.

Remove the shape from the milk carton, deflate the balloon, and cut the shape in half to form two masks.

Cheeks, noses, chins, or other features may be built up with small boxes or with tissue paper dipped in paste. The mask may be painted with tempera paint and then shellacked for durability. Bits of string, yarn, or straw may be used to decorate the painted mask; and beads or buttons can be used for eyes.

Variations and Teaching Hints

Plenty of time should be allowed for this activity. Each step in the process takes time and effort. The final result, however, is a beautiful, permanent object for the student to keep; and a great deal of learning has taken place in its creation.

Display and Storage

Finished masks may be fastened back to back on a broomstick to form a handsome totem pole for the classroom. A mask scrapbook should be prepared in advance to receive the students' creative writings.

Mask Makers

Evaluation

1. A noticeable interest in masks from many different cultures
2. A greater enthusiasm for creative writing of reports and stories
3. An appreciation of a beautiful piece of artwork

Picture the Difference

Good readers must be able to evaluate what they read; that is, they must be able to read critically. To be able to do so, a person must be able to think critically. Such reading requires an open mind, experiential background, knowledge of how and where to find information, and something about which to think. Activities that require students to compare and contrast provide them the opportunity to evaluate what they hear, see, and read.

Purposes and Objectives

1. To establish the habit of analyzing material critically
2. To give practice in reinforcing the skills of comparing and contrasting

Number of Participants

Any number

Materials Needed

☐ Art prints
☐ Photographs
☐ Magazine illustrations
☐ Several newspaper accounts of the same story
☐ Several versions of a biography
☐ Different versions of a song
☐ Brown envelopes
☐ Colored index cards
☐ Glue
☐ Cardboard

Instructions for Making Aid

1. Gather different types of visual or reading material that may be compared.
2. Glue the items to a piece of cardboard or oaktag for added durability.
3. Place two (or more) versions of the same picture, story, newspaper account, or song into a brown envelope.
4. Keep a supply of multicolored index cards available.
5. Develop activities that require students to react critically to the material.
6. Provide follow-up activities such as a discussion of professional movie review in which students may compare other viewpoints with those they have developed.

Variations and Teaching Hints

After students have analyzed a selection, have them discuss the patterns they found and indicate how it was helpful to understand the picture, story, or other item. Discuss the kinds of information usually presented in the comparison/contrast pattern: good-bad, new-old, easy-hard, expensive-inexpensive, and so forth. Have the students locate signal words that indicate comparison, such as "but," "however," "on the other hand," "still," "in comparison," and "that is."

Storage

Place the materials in envelopes decorated to have eye appeal. The envelopes can then be stored in an attractive box.

Picture the Difference

Abstract

Traditional

Evaluation

1. Ability to recognize similarities and differences
2. Participation in the activity
3. Writing and presenting unique or opposing viewpoints about an item
4. Awareness of reading terms indicating comparison

STUDENT DIRECTIONS

1. Select an envelope from the Picture the Difference box.

2. Study the material carefully.

3. On the blue card, list three things about the items that are the same.

4. On the yellow card, list three things about the items that are different.

5. On the pink card, describe which of the two items you like best and why.

6. When you have finished, fasten your cards together and place them in the envelope.

7. When ten students have completed this activity, tally your responses to find how many are alike.

Lively Limericks

Poetry is a special form of language magic. The built-in rhythm and rhyme of a well-written poem has natural appeal for almost every elementary school child. Most often, children are introduced to poetry through humorous, narrative verse; they also enjoy writing such poetry. One of the most popular forms of nonsense verse traditionally enjoyed by children is the *limerick*. It is a five-line poem in which the first, second, and fifth lines rhyme with each other. The third and fourth lines rhyme with each other and are shorter than the other three.

One of the most comprehensive collections of limericks is *The Complete Book of Nonsense*, written by Edward Lear. Although he did not actually invent the limerick, Lear did much to popularize the nonsense verse. Edward Lear did not feel a limerick was complete until he had drawn a humorous illustration for it.

The following rhyme pattern is usually found in a limerick:

Line 1 _____ a
Line 2 _____ a
Line 3 _____ b
Line 4 _____ b
Line 5 _____ a

Purposes and Objectives

1. To provide practice in using rhyming words
2. To provide incentive and reinforcement for writing creatively
3. To develop appreciation for the limerick as a poetry form

Number of Participants

Individual or small groups

Materials Needed

- [ ] Poster board
- [ ] Felt-point marker
- [ ] List of rhyming words (see Appendix K).
- [ ] Copy of *The Complete Book of Nonsense* by Edward Lear (New York: Dodd, Mead, 1946).

Directions for Making Aid

1. Construct a Lively Limerick poster similar to the one illustrated.
2. Duplicate the list of rhyming words.
3. Read limericks from *The Complete Book of Nonsense*.
4. Use an opaque projector to show Lear's nonsense drawing.
5. Ask students to write and illustrate their own limericks.

Variations and Teaching Hints

For accelerated students, an analysis of limericks should be the beginning of more difficult poetry-writing activities. Once the basic rhyme scheme of limericks has been mastered, students should be encouraged to try other and more serious forms of rhyming poetry.

Display

Display the Lively Limericks poster in a poetry center. As students write their own limericks, give them recognition by encouraging them to read the poems aloud. Place completed limericks on a bulletin board in the classroom or library.

Evaluation

1. Ability to use rhyming words effectively
2. Appreciation of the limerick form of poetry

Lively Limericks

There once was a dude from out West,
Who thought he could ride with the best;
When his horse went to jump,
He fell with a thump,
That arrogant man from out West.

STUDENT DIRECTIONS

1. Examine the Lively Limerick poster.

2. Make sure you understand the rhythm and rhyme pattern of a limerick.

3. Study the list of rhyming words.

4. Write and illustrate your own limerick.

5. Read your limerick to a friend.

6. Mount your limerick on colored paper for the bulletin board.

Bookbinding

Most publishers produce a book according to a defined system or prearranged pattern. The most commonly used format is book cover, end papers, title page, copyright page, spine, preface, table of contents, main text, appendix, and index. To engender fondness for books and to make the classroom library more personal, you can encourage students to produce their own books. Student-made books with hardcover bindings may also be used to teach the parts of a book, to promote library skills, or to preserve student writing.

Purposes and Objectives

1. Practice in recognizing the basic parts of a book
2. Motivation for preserving student writing
3. Appreciation of the aesthetics of bookbinding

Number of Participants

One to four per book

Materials Needed

- ☐ Heavy cardboard
- ☐ Cloth, contact paper, or wallpaper
- ☐ Typing paper (8½" × 11")
- ☐ Construction paper
- ☐ Large needle and heavy thread
- ☐ Masking tape
- ☐ White glue or rubber cement
- ☐ Scissors

Instructions for Making Aid

1. Decide on the size of the book and cut the materials to the appropriate size. The following measurements are suggested:

   cardboard, 5¾" × 8"
   paper, 7½" × 11"
   construction paper, 7½" × 11"

2. Place the contact paper (or other material) with the right side facedown. Place the two cardboard pieces on the wrong side so they look like an open book. Center the cardboard with one-half inch between the pieces (see illustration).

3. After leaving one inch around the outline, trim away excess contact paper.

4. Fold the corners of the contact paper neatly over the cardboard and secure them tightly.

5. Fold about eight sheets of typing paper in half and make a secure crease. Open the paper and sew two stitches along the inside fold.

6. Glue a piece of construction paper over the first and last pages, and secure them tightly to the covers of the book with white glue.

Variations and Teaching Hints

Other types of books that students may produce include the following:

   Travel journals
   Diaries
   Flip books

Photo albums

Stamp albums

Scrapbooks

Japanese style books (accordian)

Scrolls

Comic books

Nonsense books

Sketchbooks

Book of rubbings

Experimental books

STUDENT DIRECTIONS

1. Make a book using your own design, lettering, and pictures.

2. Write a title page for your story.

3. Place the title of the story on the cover.

4. Arrange the table of contents.

5. Copy your story in your book after you have written it out on notebook paper.

6. Use crayons, cut letters, string writing, colored pencils, chalk, charcoal, or paint for illustrations and lettering.

7. For variety, use finger-paint paper, tissue paper, fine stationery, construction paper, Christmas cards, rice paper, wallpaper, newspaper, and so forth.

8. Draw the illustrations for the book on a separate sheet of paper and paste them in the book.

9. Use hairspray as a fixative for your illustrations.

10. Determine the proper Dewey decimal number for your book and add it to the classroom library collection.

Students can make books as special gifts for Christmas, Mother's Day, or other holidays.

Display and Storage

Student-produced books may be prominently displayed on bookracks with the cover showing. They may also be permanently added to the library collection with process cards so they can be checked out.

Bookbinding

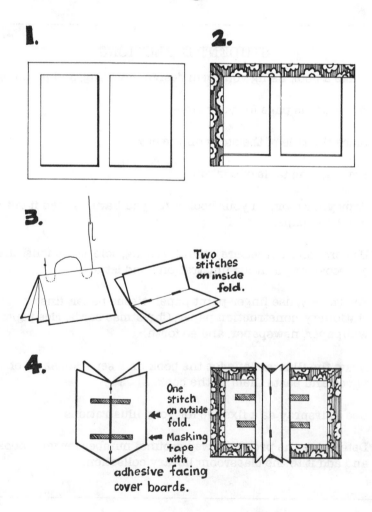

1.

2.

3.

Two stitches on inside fold.

4.

One stitch on outside fold.

Masking tape with adhesive facing cover boards.

Evaluation

1. Sustained student interest in bookbinding
2. Ability to identify parts of books
3. Interest in *personalized* writing
4. Desire to improve writing

Writing: It's in the Bag

The classroom environment can be a significant influence in helping students develop writing competence. Language arts teachers can provide unique opportunities for writing, serve as guides in the development of student writing skills, and promote various means of sharing student writing. The activity described here is suitable for use in the primary grades as students are beginning to write. It will also be useful for older students who are seeking ideas for a writing activity.

Purposes and Objectives

1. To provide practice in writing personal letters
2. To provide practice in writing news stories
3. To provide practice in writing diaries or classroom logs
4. To provide practice in writing announcements and notices

Number of Participants

One to four

Materials Needed

- ☐ Shoe bag with twelve pockets
- ☐ Assortment of writing equipment—pencils, pens, erasers
- ☐ Notepads
- ☐ Postcards
- ☐ Diary
- ☐ Index cards
- ☐ Newspapers
- ☐ Autograph book
- ☐ Cartoons

☐   Quill pen and berry ink

☐   Surprise box

☐   Pictures of class members

☐   Small toys and objects

☐   Spinner (optional)

STUDENT DIRECTIONS

1. Select a writing activity from the bag.

2. If you cannot think of a project, spin the spinner.

3. Complete the writing activity by following the instructions included in the pocket of the shoe bag.

4. Proofread your paper.

5. Share your writing with a friend and with the teacher.

Instructions for Making Aid

1. Mount a twelve-pocket shoe bag in a writing center and place a caption over the top—"Writing: It's in the Bag."

2. Gather essential materials to encourage student writing and place them in the twelve pockets.

3. Ask the students to select a writing activity or encourage them to *spin-a-project*.

4. Provide specific student directions for tasks such as the following:

    Keeping class minutes

    Writing a postcard to a friend

    Keeping a diary

    Taking notes from a book

    Writing a letter to an editor

    Creating captions for a cartoon

    Fancy writing with a quill pen and berry ink

Writing about the mystery box

Developing an outline

Writing a story about an object or toy

Variations and Teaching Hints

The writing activities should be balanced between creative and functional writing. Other activities might include the following:

CREATIVE	FUNCTIONAL
Nonsense titles	An editorial
A limerick	A biography
A ballad	Minutes of a meeting
Familiar characters	Bibliographies and footnotes
Personification	Reviews and articles
Haiku poetry	Summaries of learning experiences
A short story	Timelines
Rewriting a fairytale	Letters
What if? stories	

One good way to help students evaluate the writing is through the use of standards with which to compare their writing. Standards may be developed by the students themselves, or they may use objective standards such as the proofreader's chart.

Display

Display the shoe bag in a prominent place in the classroom or in the writing center. The shoe bag is likely to be the focal point of independent writing activities for several weeks.

Evaluation

1. Heightened interest in various writing forms and in both functional and creative types of writing

2. Increased proficiency in specific writing skills, such as spelling, grammar, and punctuation

3. Improved understanding of the steps involved in various forms of writing

Berry Ink and Quill Pen

Copies of early American documents, featuring ornate penmanship with its many flourishes, are available in most school libraries. The signatures on these documents are especially decorative. Some students might like to try fancy writing, but it should be pointed out that fancy strokes are not necessary in today's writing. According to the present trend, the plainer the writing the better, with well-formed letters, proper spacing, and consistent slant.

To help students appreciate the variety of excellent writing tools now available, you might suggest that they make their own pens and ink just as early American children did before the invention of pencils, ball-point pens, and felt-point writers. This is a simple experiment but very effective in its message.

Purposes and Objectives

1. To practice the art of fancy writing
2. To promote an awareness of different types of writing
3. To promote an appreciation for beautiful penmanship
4. To provide practice in following a sequence of directions

Number of Participants

One or two

STUDENT DIRECTIONS

1. With a sharp knife, cut the end of a feather to a sharp point (see illustration).

2. Mash a cup of ripe berries through a strainer.

3. Add a teaspoon of vinegar and a teaspoon of salt. Mix well.

4. Store in a small jar.

5. Practice dipping the quill pen in the ink and making smooth strokes without blots.

Materials Needed

- ☐ Sharp knife
- ☐ Wing feathers from a large bird (from zoos, poultry farms, or processing plants)
- ☐ One cup of blueberries, blackberries, or raspberries (either fresh or frozen)
- ☐ Kitchen strainer
- ☐ Vinegar
- ☐ Salt
- ☐ Small jar

Variations and Teaching Hints

Demonstrate other forms of fancy writing such as calligraphy. It is usually written with a special type of dip pen. Calligraphy is a graceful and artistic form of writing, and it is fairly easy to learn. A study of fancy writing would include a discussion of unique writing instruments and special alphabets. Such a study is well-suited to the interests and needs of accelerated students.

Fancy writing could also be used for special writing assignments such as those found in Writing: It's in the Bag.

Berry Ink and Quill Pen

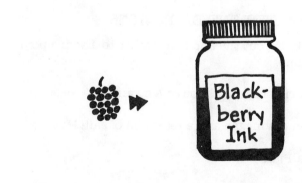

Display and Storage

Keep the berry ink and quill pen in a special place in a writing center.

Evaluation

1. Ability to follow accurately a sequence of directions
2. Interest in experimenting with the technique of fancy writing
3. An awareness of fancy writing as it was used in early America when few people knew how to write

On Your Punctuation Mark

One of the most troublesome problems in student writing is evaluation and recopying in order to achieve the perfect paper. Procedures for evaluating student writing have included marking every error with red ink to avoid any direct form of evaluation on the premise that it inhibits creativity and stifles effort. Evaluation practices aimed at improving the quality of writing should include input from both teachers and students. One means for guiding student development in writing is to promote proofreading and self-correction. This practice will allow evaluation to be an ongoing process that will become a natural, integral part of every writing experience.

Purposes and Objectives

1. To strengthen and reinforce specific writing skills
2. To promote effective proofreading and self-correction
3. To identify specific writing errors and to encourage student editing

Number of Participants

One

Materials Needed

- ☐ Cardboard or poster board
- ☐ Felt-tip marker
- ☐ Magnetic tape
- ☐ Scissors

☐ Glue

☐ Small box or other container

Instructions for Making Aid

1. Draw proofreader's symbols on small pieces of cardboard (see illustration).
2. Describe the meaning of the proofreader's symbol on the back of the card (see illustration).
3. Make at least three cards for each proofreader's symbol.
4. Fasten magnetic tape to the back of the cards. (Most chalkboards are now magnetic, and the cards will stick to the board.)
5. Place the cards in a box or other container for permanent storage.
6. Write a story containing several different types of writing errors on the chalkboard.

STUDENT DIRECTIONS

1. Read the story on the chalkboard.

2. See if there are any spelling, punctuation, or other errors in the writing.

3. Take the appropriate symbol from the container with the proofreader's symbols.

4. Place the symbol on the board at the place an error is discovered.

5. Check with the teacher to see if your proofreading is correct.

Variations and Teaching Hints

A proofreader's chart can also be used as an introduction to the symbols. After the most frequently used symbols have been mastered, additional marks may be added to the list. A complete discussion of all the proofreader's symbols and their meanings is found at the beginning of most large dictionaries.

Another way to reinforce student understanding of proofreader's symbols and to solve the problem of recopying is to use the code marks on student writing. As papers are corrected, the teacher uses proofreader's symbols to signify various errors in spelling and writing. The marks are made lightly with a soft-lead pencil in the far left margin preceding each line of text. The student then interprets the code, corrects the error, erases the teacher's marks (or with the scissors clips off the strip containing the marks), and enjoys a neat-looking corrected paper.

Display and Storage

Place the proofreader's symbols in a can or box near the chalkboard. Decorate the container attractively to remind students of the contents. If you make a large chart of basic proofreader's marks, post it in a prominent place so that students can refer to it easily.

Evaluation

1. Understanding of the basic proofreader's symbols
2. Self-correction and editing of writing

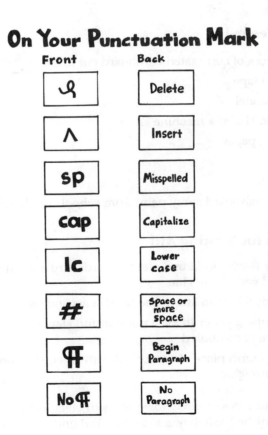

Multipurpose Board

On occasions when a table-size chalkboard is needed for a small group demonstration, a teacher-made board works very well. By constructing it with four sides, it can also be modified to serve as a magnetic board, a felt board, or a pocket chart. It can also be used by students for a variety of language arts activities.

Purposes and Objectives

1. To provide a tool for demonstrating various words, phrases, and sentences to students.
2. To provide a device that students may use independently in language arts activities

Number of Participants

One to three

Materials Needed

- ☐ Four pieces of corrugated cardboard cut in 14" × 24" pieces
- ☐ Electrical tape
- ☐ Felt or flannel
- ☐ Tin cut to size at a machine shop
- ☐ Wrapping paper
- ☐ Stapler
- ☐ White glue
- ☐ Slate or chalkboard spray paint from school supply store

Instructions for Making Aid

1. Cut felt or flannel to fit one piece of cardboard and attach it to the cardboard with white glue.
2. Use electrical tape to attach the tin to a second piece of cardboard.
3. Pleat wrapping paper to form pockets and staple it along the sides of a third piece of cardboard.
4. Spray the fourth piece of cardboard with green chalkboard paint. Allow to dry thoroughly.

Fasten all four sides securely together with electrical tape. The multipurpose board is now finished. When one side is tucked under the other, as shown in the illustration, the board stands alone with two sides exposed to form working surfaces. The board folds flat for storage.

Scraps of flannel, felt, pellon, or sandpaper will adhere to the feltboard and may be used to enrich storytelling, word study, and other activities.

Magnetic letters are available from toy shops and school supply stores. They may be combined to form words, and the words combined to form sentences. The magnetic board also lends itself to phonics activities of all kinds. Magnetic tape may be purchased by the yard to fasten to the backs of paper or cardboard cutouts.

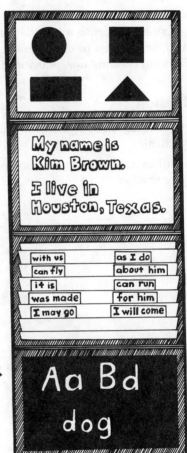

Felt

Magnetic

My name is
Kim Brown.

I live in
Houston, Texas.

Pocket

with us	as I do
can fly	about him
it is	can run
was made	for him
I may go	I will come

Chalk

Aa Bd

dog

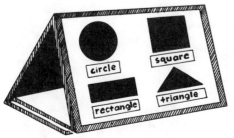

circle square

rectangle triangle

For the chalkboard side of the multipurpose board, the only accessories needed are white or colored chalk and erasers. Most schoolchildren do not have the opportunity to practice writing on the chalkboard as much as they would like, and this mini-chalkboard helps to alleviate the problem.

The pocket chart or sentence holder is used to hold word cards, pictures, or sentence strips. One of its most beneficial uses is for paragraph building, in which students add one sentence at a time to the pockets to form a meaningful paragraph.

Variations and Teaching Hints

The multipurpose board is extremely well liked by children. They never seem to tire of using it. Because it is both inexpensive and easy to make, it is possible for them to have access to one or more of the boards at all times. Allow students a free hand in creating new activities for the board.

Evaluation

1. Increasing independence in carrying out a variety of language arts activities

2. Enthusiasm in using a versatile tool for activities usually reserved for the teacher

PART III

ACTIVITIES TO ENRICH GRAMMAR AND SPELLING

A Tree for All Seasons

A small dried tree in the classroom not only provides a yearlong teaching aid, but is an object of natural beauty as well. Students attach various language elements (leaves) to the tree day by day as they are encountered. The emphasis is changed monthly to focus on different language features and also to be in keeping with each new season. Continuing activities of this type add a welcome bit of stability to the modern classroom curriculum, which has a tendency toward fragmentation.

Purposes and Objectives

1. To create an awareness of the versatility of English words
2. To encourage classification of various types of words and word patterns
3. To aid understanding of figurative language
4. To create interest in word study

Number of Participants

Any number

Materials Needed

- ☐ Dry branch (approximately three to four feet tall) with as many twigs as possible
- ☐ Large clay flowerpot
- ☐ Quick-drying plaster
- ☐ White spray paint (optional)
- ☐ Colored construction paper
- ☐ Scissors
- ☐ Paper clips
- ☐ Felt-point pen

Instructions for Making Aid

1. Wedge the branch into the flowerpot.
2. Fill the pot with wet plaster.
3. Allow to dry for several days.
4. Spray paint the tree white if desired.
5. Cover the plaster with soil or Easter grass

A Tree for All Seasons

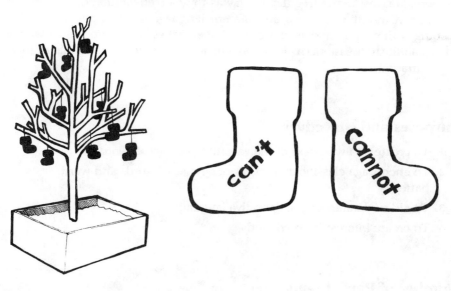

Variations and Teaching Hints

MONTH	SHAPE	LANGUAGE FEATURE
September	Autumn leaves or apples	Contractions (see Appendix G)
October	Jack-o'-lanterns or ghosts	Abbreviations (see Appendix H)
November	Turkeys or pumpkins	Synonyms
December	Stockings or stars	Antonyms (see Appendix I)
January	Snowmen and women	Homophones (see Appendix J)
February	Hearts or silhouettes of patriots	Compound words (see Appendix F)
March	Shamrocks or top hats	Common suffixes (see Appendix E)
April	Umbrellas	Common prefixes (see Appendix D)
May	Flowers	Acronyms (see Appendix L)

In supplying lists of words for students to use, the teacher may wish to refer to the appendices at the back of this book.

Each season should be introduced with a storytelling session.

STUDENT DIRECTIONS

1. Cut colored construction paper into desired shapes—Jack-o'-lanterns, hearts, and so forth.

2. Label shapes with types of words being studied—contractions, abbreviations, and so forth.

3. Hang words on the tree with paper clips.

4. Continue hanging shapes on the tree throughout the month.

Display and Storage

Provide a prominent but out-of-the-way place for the tree to stand permanently. A color photograph of the Tree for All Seasons taken at the end of each month will make an excellent addition to the class scrapbook.

Evaluation

1. Increased proficiency in the use of various language features
2. Accuracy in spelling the words emphasized in the activity
3. Interest in language study

Paper Folding

The art of paper folding has been a popular pastime of adults and children alike for hundreds of years. Because it is such a pleasant diversion, it has value in vocabulary development when incorporated into the language arts program.

For primary children, the best and least expensive paper for folding is plain mimeograph paper. Both white and pastel colors may be used for variety.

In paper folding, the number of possible shapes is practically endless; but for our purposes, only three examples will be given.

Purposes and Objectives

1. To afford variety and interest in the process of word building
2. To provide an independent art activity for young children
3. To give practice in using the dictionary

Number of Participants

Any number

Materials Needed

- ☐ Mimeograph paper in white and pastel colors
- ☐ Picture dictionaries
- ☐ Scissors
- ☐ Black felt-point pen
- ☐ Shoe boxes for storage

Paper Folding

1.

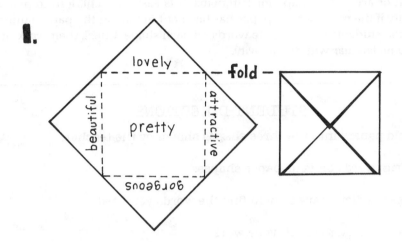

2.

3.

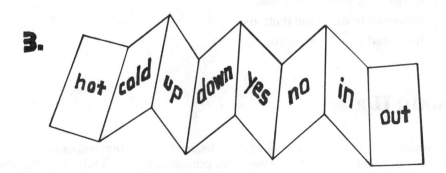

Instructions for Making Aid

Provide materials and demonstrate the folding of the three basic shapes shown: (1) the four-fold square for synonyms, (2) the tri-fold for compound words, and (3) the fan or accordian shape for antonyms. It is easier for children to manage this activity if the mimeograph paper has been cut in half on the paper cutter.

Show the students how to write words on each shape. Check their work until they become familiar with the activity.

STUDENT DIRECTIONS

1. Fold papers into the three shapes shown by the teacher.

2. Write words on your paper shapes.

3. Use the dictionary to help find the words you need.

4. Ask a friend to check your work.

5. Put your shapes in the box for others to read.

Variations and Teaching Hints

This activity is well suited to accelerated students who may proceed with the vocabulary as far as they have the ability and inclination to go. The activity should be continued for six to eight weeks since students will be working independently at their leisure.

Evaluation

1. Evidence of wider word usage
2. Efficiency in using the dictionary
3. Increased interest in words

Noun House

As students gain a wider vocabulary, they begin to realize that words may be used in many different ways and for a variety of purposes. Students form classifications for words: some are used for naming or labeling, some to show action, and still others to modify or change words.

Although *parts of speech* should always be presented and taught in context, within sentences or phrases, there is a place for practicing these words in isolation; and such practice is more effective when provided as an independent activity in a game format.

The Noun House activity provides practice in isolating nouns from an assortment of words containing both nouns and other parts of speech.

Purposes and Objectives

1. To strengthen and reinforce sight words
2. To help students identify common nouns, proper nouns, and verbs

Number of Participants

One to four

Noun/Verb House

roof

fold line

carton

side pieces

end pieces

Cut two of each

1" folds around both ends

Report cover sliding spine secures roof

Nouns
Only nouns live here.

Materials Needed

☐ One cardboard six-pack drink carton

☐ One sheet of lightweight poster board

☐ One pack of 3″ × 5″ index cards

☐ Black felt-point pen

☐ Scissors

☐ Paste

Instructions for Making Aid

1. Remove the dividers from inside the carton.

2. Cover the outside of the carton with colored paper.

3. Paste on doors and windows to give the appearance of a house.

4. Cut a piece of poster board and fold it in half to form a removable roof for the house.

5. Label the roof as follows: "Nouns: Only nouns live here."

6. Label each index card with a word being studied by students. Use both nouns and other parts of speech.

7. Prepare a key of correct answers.

STUDENT DIRECTIONS

1. Shuffle the word cards.

2. Place the deck facedown on the table.

3. Draw a card and read the word aloud.

4. If the word is a noun, lift the roof and place it inside the house.

5. If the word is not a noun, place it on the bottom of the deck.

6. Check the answer key. If the player is correct, place a tally mark by his or her name.

7. Continue taking turns until all nouns are in the Noun House.

8. The player with the most tally marks wins.

Variations and Teaching Hints

Several sets of cards should be prepared to add variety to this game and to teach more words. Verbs and proper nouns may be used instead of common nouns by labeling the roof appropriately. A corresponding foreign word may be added to each card for students who are learning English as a second language.

Storage

Store card packs, along with the key to each one, inside the Noun House. Students choose the deck they will use.

Evaluation

1. Increase in sight vocabulary reflected in more fluent reading
2. Ability to identify common nouns, proper nouns, and verbs

Chief Spellum Chart

Many students have not developed a systematic plan for learning to spell a new word. Either they do not know the proper procedure to follow or they are not in the habit of using a systematic approach.

The illustration for this activity is based on learning theory but is presented in graphic form to make the process appealing and practical for elementary school students.

Purposes and Objectives

1. To give students a systematic plan for studying the spelling of a word
2. To develop greater efficiency in spelling usage

Number of Participants

Any number

Materials Needed

- ☐ White poster board
- ☐ Tempera paint
- ☐ Brushes
- ☐ Stick-on letters (or felt-point pen for hand lettering)

Instructions for Making Aid

Use an opaque projector to enlarge the illustration. Transfer the design to white poster paper and paint it in bright colors. Print the directions in large black letters on white for easy reading. Laminate the finished chart and post it near the children at their eye level.

Variations and Teaching Hints

To help students develop the habit of using the spelling procedure, "walk" them through the steps several times. Keep the chart posted and review it occasionally.

Evaluation

1. Evidence of improved spelling on weekly tests
2. Evidence of improved spelling in everyday writing tasks

STUDENT DIRECTIONS

1. Open your spelling book to the right lesson.

2. Have your paper and pencil ready.

3. Study the Chief Spellum chart.

4. Follow the steps in order as you study each word.

Spelling Progress Chart

When students keep a personal record of spelling progress, they tend to make greater gains in spelling achievement than when no graphic record is kept. Many language arts teachers have found that a bar graph, on which students plot weekly test scores, is a successful method of illustrating to students and their parents how well basal spelling words are being learned.

Purposes and Objectives

1. To illustrate progress over a period of time
2. To encourage maximum effort in learning basal spelling words
3. To create a lasting interest in spelling competency

Number of Participants

Any number

Materials Needed

☐ Copies of the grid on page 110 (one per student)

☐ Spiral notebooks (one per student)

☐ Crayons or map pencils

Instructions for Making Aid

Staple a grid inside the back cover of each spiral notebook and issue a notebook to each student. Administer a weekly test for required basal spelling words. Have students take the test in their notebooks. Correct the words and provide exercises on any misspelled words. Ask students to record their weekly scores on the grid.

Variations and Teaching Hints

By adapting the spelling words to fit groups of children, you can use this plan for positive reinforcement at any level. Some students may need to have the words presented in a foreign language as well as in English.

When the record sheet is completed, a new one may be stapled over the old Thus, the notebook becomes a running account of spelling achievement. It contains all tests, practice exercises, and the record of progress.

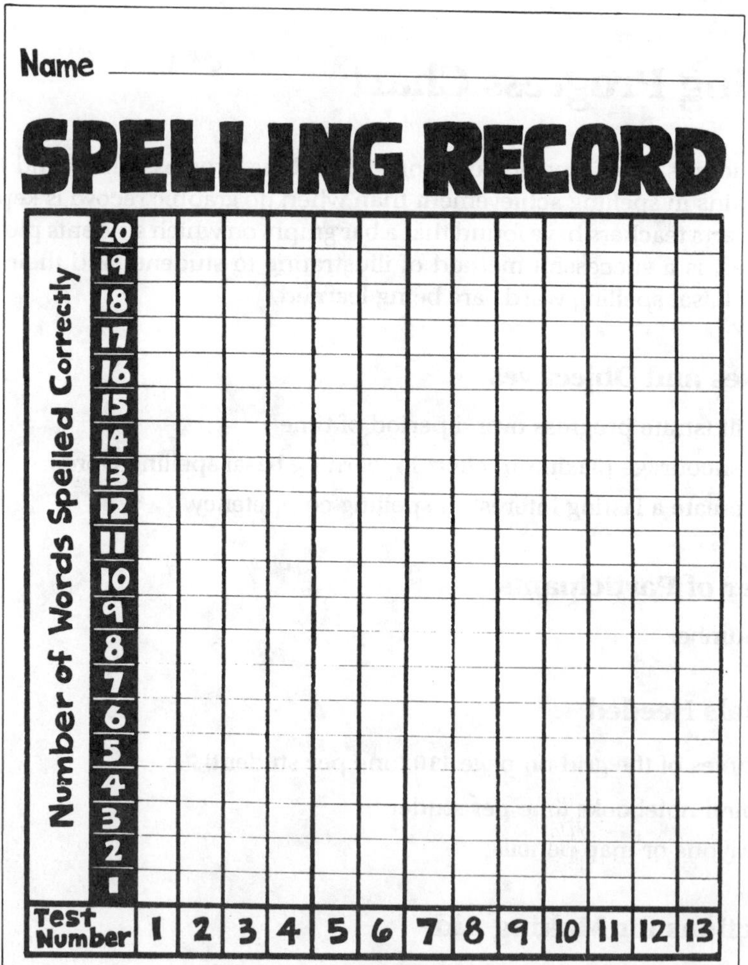
Name ____________________

SPELLING RECORD

Number of Words Spelled Correctly: 20 19 18 17 16 15 14 13 12 11 10 9 8 7 6 5 4 3 2 1

Test Number: 1 2 3 4 5 6 7 8 9 10 11 12 13

STUDENT DIRECTIONS

1. Write your name on the cover of your spelling notebook.

2. Write your name on the spelling record at the back.

3. Study the spelling words in your textbook.

4. Write your test words in the notebook.

5. Correct your test.

6. Study any words not spelled correctly.

7. Date your test and the record sheet.

8. Color in a square for each word you spelled correctly.

Evaluation

1. Improvement in spelling, from one week to the next, shown on the record sheets

2. Evidence of improved attitudes toward studying basal spelling words

3. Greater accuracy in spelling in everyday writing tasks

Holiday Vocabulary Charts

Nouns that students are likely to be using in holiday stories, letters, and poems should be made accessible to them in various ways. A chart similar to the one on page 113 may be prepared for each holiday of the school year and posted several weeks prior to the holiday.

For word acquisition and spelling, each noun should be printed in large black letters on white or buff chart paper and illustrated with a small rebus picture. Pictures may be cut from old readiness books or from magazines, or they may be hand drawn.

An excellent reference book to use in developing vocabulary is *Christmas in America*, written and illustrated by Lillie Patterson (Champaign, Ill.' Garrard, 1969).

It is one of a series of holiday books, clearly written and vividly illustrated for use by children and teachers. It contains legends, lore, and symbolism of the holiday. The following are other titles in the series:

Fourth of July	Patriots' Days
Thanksgiving	Valentine's Day
Halloween	Birthdays
Spring Holidays	Poetry for Holidays
New Year's Day	Easter

Purposes and Objectives

1. To help students write effectively by providing some of the words they may need
2. To enrich vocabulary and improve spelling

Number of Participants

Any number

Materials Needed

☐ Lined chart paper

☐ Black felt-point pen (wide nib)

☐ Small pictures

☐ Paste

Instructions for Making Aid

Use reference books to prepare a list of words appropriate to each holiday. Print the words in columns on chart paper and illustrate each word. Prepare a large scrapbook in which students may display their finished writing.

Variations and Teaching Hints

The noun list suggested in the illustration should be supplemented with words from dictionaries and lists of basic sight words (see Appendix A). For students who are studying English as a second language, the holiday words may be printed in both languages. The charts may be laminated and used year after year.

Evaluation

When the holiday season is over, a paper-and-pencil test or an oral spelling review may be used to determine how many seasonal words the students have learned.

STUDENT DIRECTIONS

1. Write a story about the holiday we celebrate this month.

2. Use the word chart to help you with spelling.

3. Ask someone to proofread your writing.

4. Make a picture for your story.

5. Paste your story in the holiday scrapbook.

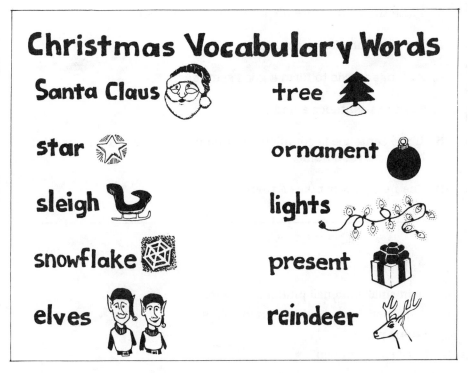

Sentence Building Blocks

In the Sentence Building Blocks activity, proper nouns, verbs, articles, and common nouns are combined in various ways to provide practice in sentence formation and recognition of parts of speech.

Purposes and Objectives

1. To provide a basic understanding of sentence structure
2. To give practice on sight words
3. To develop familiarity with four parts of speech

Number of Participants

One to four

STUDENT DIRECTIONS

1. Place the word cubes on a desk or on the floor.

2. Set the timer for one minute.

3. Arrange words to form a good sentence.

4. Read the sentence aloud.

5. If the sentence is completed in one minute, place a tally mark by the player's name.

6. The next player takes a turn.

Materials Needed

- ☐ Eight small (one-half pint) milk cartons
- ☐ Construction papers in assorted colors
- ☐ Typing paper
- ☐ Black felt-point pen

☐ Glue

☐ Egg timer

Instructions for Making Aid

1. Trim the tops off two milk cartons and slip one inside the other to form a cube.

2. Cover each cube with construction paper, using a different color for each part of speech.

3. Make a separate cube for each part of speech.

4. Print words from the Basic Blocks list on white paper and glue to the six sides.

BASIC BLOCKS

PROPER NOUNS	VERBS	ARTICLES	COMMON NOUNS
Andi	finds	a	ball
Father	gets	one	book
Amy	likes	that	boat
Mother	sees	that	game
Pete	takes	the	dog
Betty	wants	this	toy

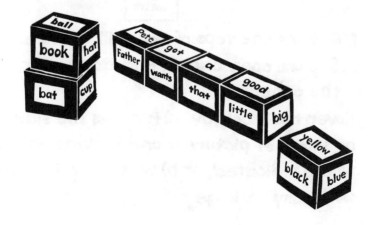

Sentence Building Blocks

Variations and Teaching Hints

Make up several sets of blocks using different words from the noun list (see Appendix B) and proper names, for example, the names of the children in the class. Cubes containing adjectives and adverbs may be added for more mature readers. For children learning English as a second language, each word may be accompanied by its foreign equivalent. The activity may be made more challenging for accelerated students by making the blocks all the same color.

Storage

Sets of word cubes are best stored in brown paper bags and numbered for identification.

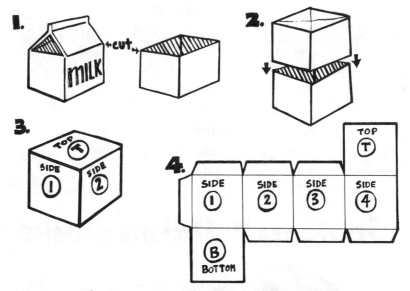

1. Cut off the tops of two milk cartons.

2. Slip one open carton end down over the other.

Cover the block by a) tracing the sides as shown in picture 4 and leaving ½" flaps where indicated, or b) wrapping it as you would any package.

Evaluation

1. Awareness of parts of a sentence
2. Understanding of sentence structure
3. Practice on sight words

Noun Password

The game of Noun Password is based on the idea that one word is related to many others. This game provides an opportunity for the reader to associate many different words with frequently encountered nouns. R. Van Allen has developed a list of 230 of the most commonly used nouns in elementary reading. These words are identified as those most often encountered by primary and intermediate grade students in their textbooks and independent reading. Games such as Noun Password help young readers sharpen their ability to relate one word to another.

Purposes and Objectives

1. To give practice in recognizing the most commonly used nouns
2. To develop recognition of the noun as a meaning unit
3. To give practice in relating one noun to another

Number of Participants

Two or four

Materials Needed

- ☐ Dark construction paper
- ☐ Poster board or cardboard
- ☐ White glue
- ☐ Allen list of frequently used nouns (see Appendix B)

Instructions for Making Aid

1. Cut at least twenty pieces of cardboard according to the pattern (see illustration).
2. Randomly select eight nouns from the Allen list.

3. Write the nouns on the cards with a colored marker.

4. Using dark construction paper, make four sleeves for the noun cards.

5. For added durability, laminate the sleeves and the noun cards.

Variations and Teaching Hints

Other words may be used in place of those in the Allen noun list. See the appendices for Wilson's list and lists of antonyms, synonyms, and homonyms. A variation in the basic game is the "lightning" round. In this version, each team is given a specified length of time (one minute) to see how many words may be guessed. In another version of play, the same word list is given to both teams.

Storage

The noun cards and the sleeves should be kept in a box or envelope for easy access.

Evaluation

1. Recognition of nouns as naming words

2. Accuracy in relating one noun to another

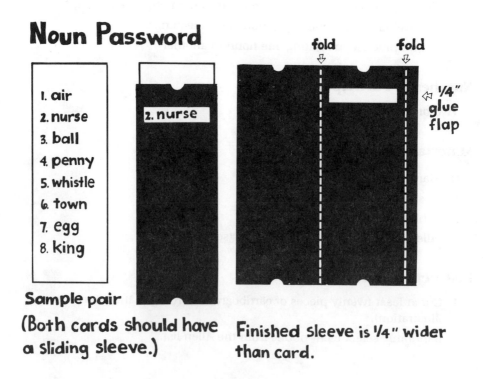

Noun Password

1. air
2. nurse
3. ball
4. penny
5. whistle
6. town
7. egg
8. king

Sample pair
(Both cards should have a sliding sleeve.)

2. nurse

fold   fold

¼" glue flap

Finished sleeve is ¼" wider than card.

STUDENT DIRECTIONS

1. Select teams of two players each.

2. Take a noun card with eight key words and place it in the holder.

3. Give a clue to a partner who tries to guess the word.

4. If your partner guesses the word correctly, your team scores a point.

5. If your partner misses the word, the other team gives the next word clue.

6. Rotate play until the word is guessed correctly.

7. The team that correctly identifies the word goes first with the next word clue.

8. The first team to reach a set number of points is the winner.

Syllaboat Sail

The ability to divide an unknown word into syllables is essential to reading because the syllable is a basic unit of pronunciation. A *syllable* is a group of letters containing one vowel sound. The sound that a letter represents often depends on its position. For example, in the words "rip" and "ripen," the addition of a syllable changes the pronunciation of the vowel. Syllabication is also an aid for accurate spelling and effective writing.

Purposes and Objectives

1. To help students understand the concept of a syllable
2. To reinforce the skill of dividing words into syllables

Number of Participants

Two to four

Materials Needed

- ☐ Game board (see illustration)
- ☐ Small sailboat tokens (see illustration)
- ☐ Deck of word cards

Instructions for Making Aid

1. Make a game board like the one illustrated.
2. Cut out tokens in the form of sailboats or use plastic boats of different colors.
3. Produce a deck of at least forty words of varying difficulty. These words may be taken from spelling or vocabulary lists.
4. Divide the word into syllables on the back of the card.

Variations and Teaching Hints

Extra spaces may be placed on the board by attaching labels such as "move ahead," "lose a turn," and so forth. Also, the spaces could be color coded with a choice of a regular or challenge word. If the student gets a correct response to a challenge word, he may receive an extra "gust of wind" and move ahead another one, two, or three squares. Change the cards or have several sets available to avoid monotony. The students may make their own word cards from stories or reading lessons.

Pattern for cardboard token.

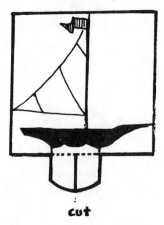

cut

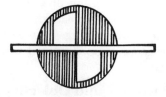

Tape token to coin.

Display and Storage

The game should be stored in an attractive box wtih a sailboat picture and should be made available as part of a language center.

Evaluation

1. Recognition of syllables

2. Increased recognition of nouns

3. Improved phonic analysis skills

STUDENT DIRECTIONS

1. Place the cards faceup in a pile.

2. Draw a card and move one space for each syllable correctly pronounced.

3. Check your answers by reversing the card.

4. Go back to the original spot if your answer is incorrect.

5. The first sailboat to reach the pirate's treasure wins the game.

Grammar "500"

Many teachers believe that current methods of teaching the parts of speech in the elementary classroom are too formal and abstract. Despite the fact that grammar instruction is difficult, there is a need to emphasize it as an essential language arts skill. Because instruction in traditional grammar continues to stress the classification of words into the eight parts of speech, a task that is difficult for many children, it is important that the teacher make instruction interesting.

Objectives and Purposes

1. To give practice in understanding and identifying the parts of speech

2. To reinforce the concept that words perform many different functions in a sentence

Number of Participants

Two to four

Materials Needed

- ☐ Poster board
- ☐ Tokens or matchbox cars
- ☐ Deck of thirty-six index cards

Instructions for Making Aid

1. Use an opaque projector to enlarge the diagram to approximately 22″ × 28.″
2. Make a deck of thirty-six cards and write words of varying difficulty on them.
3. Make (or buy) four race car tokens.
4. Make an answer key identifying the correct part of speech for each word.
5. Place the answer key in an envelope.

STUDENT DIRECTIONS

1. Place your car on "start."

2. Shuffle the deck of cards and place them facedown.

3. Take the top card and read the word.

4. Use the word in a sentence and tell what part of speech it is. If necessary, refer to the answer key to check your response. If you are correct, move to the next square.

5. If your answer is wrong, don't move your car ahead.

6. Any player may challenge another player's answer. If correct, the challenger moves ahead three spaces. If incorrect, the challenger is forced to make a pit stop and loses a turn.

7. The first car to cross the finish line is the winner.

Variations and Teaching Hints

Have students play the game with all eight parts of speech or with a limited number—nouns, verbs, adverbs, and adjectives. Another variation involves writing the word in a sentence and underlining the one you wish students to identify. When this variation is played, the correct answer should be made available so that students can check their answers. A corresponding foreign word may be added if the student is learning English as a foreign language.

Evaluation

1. Recognition of parts of speech in context
2. Increased understanding that many words are misunderstood if used incorrectly
3. Improved student vocabulary
4. Interest in the game

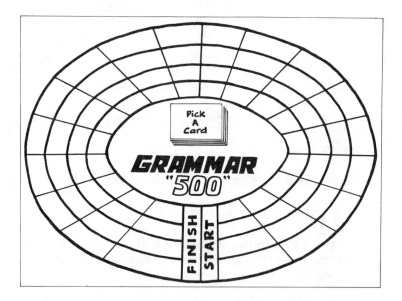

Car Capers

The individualized learning packet is a useful tool in structuring and in organizing related instructional activities. A well-made learning packet usually contains three essential elements: (1) a succinctly stated instructional objective, (2) the criteria for acceptable performance, and (3) the directions to accomplish a specific task.

Individualized learning packets are easily adapted to a variety of classroom environments. Included here is a teacher-made learning packet suitable for use with upper grade elementary students.

Purposes and Objectives

1. To reinforce various components of grammar and writing
2. To give practice in identifying parts of speech found in commercial writing
3. To give practice in writing a paragraph that contains a topic sentence, a controlling idea, and a conclusion

Materials Needed

- ☐ Cardboard box
- ☐ Pictures of automobiles
- ☐ Automobile advertisements
- ☐ Felt-point marking pens
- ☐ Large envelope
- ☐ Cardboard or poster board
- ☐ Clear contact paper

Number of Participants

Individual or small group

Instructions for Making Aid

1. Construct a cardboard Car Capers box (see illustration).
2. Glue pictures of cars on the box.
3. Produce individual grammar and writing activities around the theme of automobiles. Included here are a few examples.

Plurals and possessives. Collect ads from various automobile dealers. Ask the student to scan the brochures, to list the names of ten different cars, and to write the plural and possessive form for each name beside each car.

Parts of speech. Ask the student to circle all of the nouns (common and proper), pronouns, and adjectives used in a car advertisement. The student then constructs a bar graph indicating the frequency of use for each part of speech.

Etymology (word origin). Ask the student to look up the history and backgrounds of various automobile names. The list should include both foreign and domestic types—Chevrolet, Omni, Volkswagen, Lynx, and so forth. Interesting information about the origins of such names is found in the dictionary, encyclopedia, atlas.

Synonyms. Ask the student to list, on 3" × 5" cards, adjectives and adverbs used in automobile ads. On the back of each card, the student could write one (or more) synonyms for the found word.

Sentence structure. Ask the student to print sentences from an automobile ad on sentence strips and to cut the sentence strips apart between the noun phrase and verb phrase. The student then checks to see if any of the phrases are interchangeable and creates several new sentences.

Sentence expansion. Have the student look through automobile literature to find simple, declarative sentences, such as "The car stopped." The student then illustrates ways that such sentences may be expanded into more descriptive ones, such as "The sporty Trans Am stopped at the pit for a quick transfusion of oil."

Paragraph expansion. Ask the student to examine the paragraph construction used in automobile brochures and to identify such features as the topic sentence, controlling idea, and conclusion. Ask the student to write a paragraph that might follow the one that was analyzed.

4. Write the directions for the activity on poster board and laminate with clear contact paper.

5. Place all necessary materials for completing the activity in a large brown envelope.

6. Label and number the individual envelopes.

STUDENT DIRECTIONS

1. Select the appropriate activity from the Car Capers box.

2. Complete the activity as directed.

3. After you complete each activity, check your answers with the teacher.

Variations and Teaching Hints

Many different activities can be developed to add variety and to teach different language arts skills. All activities should be modified so that they fit the motif of automobile advertising. Other variations on the Car Capers theme might include the following: (1) researching (finding the answers to specific questions about automobiles), (2) sequencing (listing the steps in changing a tire), (3) writing (reviewing several books on cars from both past and future). These activities are recommended for accelerated students but can be modified to meet the needs of a mainstreamed child.

Display and Storage

Provide a prominent place for individualized learning packets in a materials center.

Evaluation

1. Completion of activities in the individual learning packets
2. Increased proficiency in various grammar and writing activities
3. Ability to complete a self-directed activity

Crossword Puzzles

Crossword puzzles, sentence games, and word searches are very popular with intermediate grade teachers for strengthening reading skills or reinforcing vocabulary. However, commercially produced puzzles often have little relationship to the vocabulary students are actually studying. Word games, particularly crossword puzzles, directly associated with a subject or topic being studied in the classroom will better reinforce student understanding of words and terms used in context. It is not difficult to prepare crossword puzzles for use in vocabulary building or for subject areas being studied.

Purposes and Objectives

1. To increase student vocabulary using context clues
2. To provide spelling practice on words previously introduced
3. To reinforce specific reading skills such as structural analysis

Number of Participants

Any number

Materials Needed

- ☐ Graph or crossword puzzle model
- ☐ Word list
- ☐ Clues for crossword puzzle
- ☐ Answer sheet
- ☐ Pencils

Instructions for Making Aid

1. Construct a master crossword puzzle form to use for many different purposes. You can use graph paper or the illustrated model.
2. Develop a list of words that you want to introduce, teach, or reinforce. The selected words should be from a single source, perhaps from textbook material presently being studied. Words that are related to one another will be more meaningful to the students.
3. Place the longest words in the center of the puzzle either horizontally or vertically. Use fifteen to twenty words in a 15 × 15 grid.
4. Develop the clues—approximately the same number across and down.

5. Transfer the blank puzzle and word clues to a ditto sheet or use a photocopy machine for easy duplication.

6. Make an answer key so that students may check their answers.

STUDENT DIRECTIONS

1. After reading a story or other assignment, complete the crossword puzzle.

2. Use a pencil when working on a crossword puzzle. You may wish to change your answer.

3. Print the answers in capital letters. They are easier to read.

4. Work on the crossword puzzle for about fifteen minutes. Check your answers with the key.

Crossword Puzzle Frame

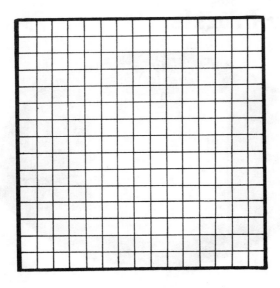

Variations and Teaching Hints

Several different crossword puzzles should be developed to add variety and teach additional skills. You should vary the way the clues are structured to provide additional practice in different language arts skills. Included here are several variations for presenting crossword puzzle clues:

1. Place a word list or word bank for all of the words in the puzzle at the bottom of the page.

2. Create the crossword puzzle clues using the *cloze* procedure, for example, "Plant seeds in rich _____."

3. Scramble the puzzle words in the clue, for example, "Check books out from the BRYLAIR."

4. Produce other types of word puzzles, such as word searches, cross-outs, or anagrams.

If a student does not get 75 percent of the answers correct, the puzzle is probably too difficult. A warm-up session would assist students with difficult words.

Display and Storage

Place the crossword puzzles, along with the key for each one, inside a folder with the specific skill or story identified. Store the folders inside a cardboard box covered with crossword puzzles clipped from newspapers, and place the box in a learning center or other convenient area.

Pigskin Puzzle

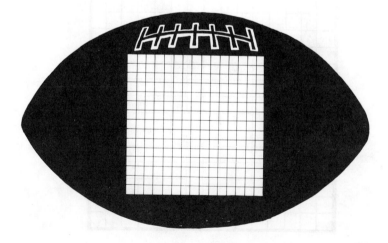

Evaluation

1. Completion of the puzzle in a specified period of time
2. Ability to correctly identify most of the word clues
3. Student self-correction or nongraded teacher evaluation
4. Evaluation of a completed puzzle during a teacher-student conference

Cat Skills

ACROSS

CLUES FOR "CAT SKILLS"

2. First note of the musical scale
4. The sound a cat makes
6. "_____ apple a day . . ."
8. A single sound of music
9. Name for a male cat
11. Seventh note of the scale
12. Money
16. Space
17. A baby cat

DOWN

1. Cap
3. Opposite of "off"
4. Myself
5. "When you _____upon a star . . ."
7. The long form of don't is do _____.
10. A drink you get from a cow
12. A dog or _____ makes a good pet.
13. A painting
14. Your eyes do this
15. A part of the body
18. Sick
19. The foot of a cat
20. A tool used to chop wood

PART IV

ACTIVITIES TO ENRICH SPEAKING

Classroom Cookery

Children are fascinated by the food they eat; yet they know very little about its origin, preparation, or preservation. The fact that they do have strong feelings about food and actually understand so little about it makes cooking a natural area for teaching.

Storytellers were creating and telling tales about food long before stories were recorded in print. Old folk tales were filled with the problems of earning bread and of imaginary tables loaded with rich and exotic foods.

The language arts skills of reading, writing, speaking, and listening may be strengthened when cooking in the classroom springs naturally from a piece of literature that focuses on food. *Stone Soup* by Marcia Brown (New York: Scribner's, 1947) is the retelling of a French folk tale about a large pot of vegetable soup— enough to feed an entire village. A language arts unit built around *Stone Soup* can give children an opportunity to study a fine book, to read directions in the form of a recipe, to discuss the cooking activity, and to write their reactions to the experience. Thus, all language arts skills are employed.

Purposes and Objectives

1. To give practice in literal comprehension as students read to follow directions

2. To provide an opportunity to study the elements of an authentic folk tale

3. To develop creative writing skills

Number of Participants

Any number

Materials Needed

- □ Copy of *Stone Soup* by Marcia Brown
- □ Rebus recipe chart prepared in advance (see illustration)
- □ Electric deep cooker
- □ Ground meat and vegetables for soup (may be contributed by students on a voluntary basis)
- □ Plastic knives for peeling vegetables
- □ Paper cups and plastic spoons for serving soup
- □ Round, smooth stone (optional)

Instructions for Making Aid

1. Read *Stone Soup* aloud to students.
2. Post rebus recipe chart.
3. Appoint committees for preparing vegetables.

STUDENT DIRECTIONS

1. Discuss the meaning of the folk tale *Stone Soup*.

2. Discuss the purpose of the stone in the soup.

3. Study the recipe chart.

4. Prepare vegetables for cooking.

5. Cook the soup as the chart tells you to do. Add the stone if you wish.

6. Serve the soup and enjoy your good cooking.

7. Write your feelings about the story and the soup.

8. Make a picture to go with your writing.

Variations and Teaching Hints

Safety precautions should be taken when food preparation is in progress. Plastic knives with serrated edges are used to cut vegetables and children are taught to clean up spills promptly. When food is hot and electrical appliances are being used, the teacher or aide should closely supervise all work. Safety precautions learned in the classroom can carry over into later life.

Most countries have developed stories featuring their favorite regional foods; and the study of such tales in the classroom helps to broaden students' horizons and give them a world mindedness. The following list suggests books and the foods they feature.*

The Poppy Seed Cakes by Margery Clark, (Doubleday, 1924) (cookies)

Blueberries for Sal by Robert McCloskey (Viking, 1948) (blueberry muffins)

Chicken Soup with Rice by Maurice Sendak (Harper & Row, 1962) (soup)

Bread and Jam for Frances by Russell Hoban and Lillian Hoban (Harper & Row, 1964) (toast and jam)

Old Black Witch by Wende and Harry Devlin (Parents' Magazine Press, 1963) (blueberry pancakes)

Cranberry Thanksgiving by Wende Devlin and Harry Devlin (Parents' Magazine Press, 1971) (cranberry bread)

The Duchess Bakes a Cake by Virginia Kahl (Scribner's, 1953) (1-2-3-4 cake)

The Gingerbread Man by Ed Arno (Scholastic Book Services, 1967) (gingerbread men)

Journey Cake, Ho! by Ruth Sawyer (Viking, 1953) (corn cakes)

Nail Soup by Harve Zemach (Follett, 1964) (soup)

The Egg Tree by Katherine Milhous (Scribner's, 1950) (boiled eggs)

Rain Makes Applesauce by Julian Scheer (Holiday House, 1964) (applesauce)

Five O'Clock Charlie by Marguerite Henry (Rand McNally, 1962) (apple tarts)

Mr. Rabbit and the Lovely Present by Charlotte Zolotow (Harper & Row, 1962) (fruit salad)

The Funny Little Woman by Arlene Mosel (E. P. Dutton, 1972) (rice balls)

Strega Nona by Tomie de Paola (Prentice-Hall, 1975) (spaghetti)

For recipes, instructional units, and teaching suggestions see Using Literature with Young Children *by* Betty Coody (Dubuque, Iowa: Brown, 1978).

Evaluation

1. Evidence of increasing ability to follow printed directions
2. Improvement in disucssion and conversation skills
3. Increasing interest in folk literature
4. An awareness of satire in literature

Earth, Sea, and Sky Frieze

A classroom frieze consists of a long, narrow band of paper on which numerous objects and figures made by children have been pasted. Frieze making provides practice in painting, cutting, and pasting and also gives children valuable experience in discussing, planning, and organizing a project. But, best of all, frieze making gives them a chance to create something of beauty.

To enhance a study of transportation, making a colorful frieze is an excellent learning experience for young children. The class should be divided into three groups representing land, water, and air travel. After a study of transportation vehicles, students are given an opportunity to depict them in art form by using crayons, colored chalk, cut paper, or tempera paint. All shapes are then cut out and pasted on the background. For vocabulary and spelling purposes, the teacher may wish to label each shape.

Purposes and Objectives

1. To encourage the study of library books on transportation
2. To foster oral language
3. To engage students in a creative group project

Number of Participants

Any number

STUDENT DIRECTIONS

1. Think of all the ways you might travel in the sky, on land, and on water.

2. Make pictures of some of the vehicles you named.

3. Cut out each shape.

4. Paste each shape on the frieze where it belongs.

5. Write a story about the project.

6. Title your story "Earth, Sea, and Sky."

Materials Needed

- ☐ Three four-yard strips of colored wrapping paper in blue, brown, and green
- ☐ Wheat paste (wallpaper paste)
- ☐ Construction paper
- ☐ Crayons, colored chalk, colored felt-point pens, and tempera paint
- ☐ Scissors
- ☐ One-pound coffee can
- ☐ Six one-inch paint brushes (for paste)

Instructions for Making Aid

Attach the wrapping paper to a bulletin board with blue at the top to form the sky, brown in the middle to form the land, and green below to represent the sea. Mix the paste and place it near the bulletin board. The background is now ready for students to paste on various images of transportation and travel. Students should be encouraged to draw and paint as many shapes as they can think of.

Variations and Teaching Hints

To encourage vocabulary development and spelling, the teacher may label each object on the frieze. If some members of the class are bilingual, images may be labeled in two languages.

The following books contain a variety of characters that make good subjects for friezes:

Swimmy by Leo Leonni (Pantheon, 1963) (fish)

Make Way for Ducklings by Robert McCloskey (Viking, 1941) (ducks)

Millions of Cats by Wanda Gag (Coward-McCann, 1928) (cats)

Where the Wild Things Are by Maurice Sendak (Harper & Row, 1963) (monsters)

The 500 Hats of Bartholomew Cubbins by Dr. Seuss (Vanguard, 1938) (hats)

Burt Dow: Deep Water Man by Robert McCloskey (Viking, 1963) (whales)

Rabbit Hill by Robert Lawson (Viking, 1945) (rabbits)

Evaluation

1. Improved skill in oral language
2. Ability to plan and carry out a group project cooperatively
3. Accuracy in spelling nouns in creative writing related to the project

Earth, Sea, and Sky Frieze

Jigsaw Puzzles

All children enjoy jigsaw puzzles, especially those they make themselves. Puzzles may be used by the language arts teacher to strengthen both the speaking and listening skills of young children.

Purposes and Objectives

1. To provide a topic for effective oral language and listening
2. To give students a creative craft experience

Number of Participants

One to four

Materials Needed

- □ Art prints or magazine pictures of landscapes
- □ Tagboard or tablet backs
- □ Wheat paste (wallpaper paste)
- □ Scissors
- □ Black felt-point pen
- □ Chart paper

Instructions for Making Aid

Trim a landscape (or seascape) picture and tagboard backing to the same size. Paste the picture on the tagboard. Allow it to dry thoroughly. On the back, draw three horizontal and three vertical wavy lines (see illustration). With scissors, cut on the wavy lines to form twelve puzzle pieces. The puzzle is complete and ready to be reassembled.

To encourage rich oral vocabulary and careful listening, make a chart with the following questions:

If I were in this place

What sounds would I hear?

What sights would I see?

What scents would I smell?

What thoughts would I think?

What feelings would I have?

Post the chart near the areas where students will be working with puzzles. When a puzzle is put together, ask each student who worked on the puzzle to answer each question in the most descriptive way possible. Encourage others in the group to listen for unique and creative descriptive terms.

STUDENT DIRECTIONS

1. Select a puzzle from the box.

2. Put the puzzle together.

3. Study the picture.

4. Answer the questions.

5. Ask a friend to listen to your answers.

6. Check off the puzzle on the record chart.

Variations and Teaching Hints

Puzzles may be made more challenging by adding more wavy lines on the back, thus making more pieces. Puzzles should be stored in envelopes and numbered so that students can keep track of the ones they have completed. Make a puzzle record chart consisting of a bar graph that contains the names of the students and of the puzzles (see page 110). Keeping a record encourages students to complete each puzzle in the set.

Evaluation

1. Enriched oral language
2. Effective listening to oral descriptions
3. Interest in making and completing the puzzles

Jigsaw Puzzles

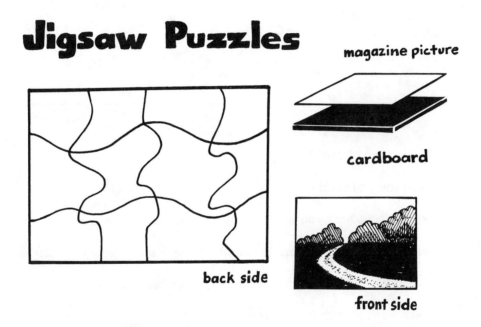

magazine picture

cardboard

back side

front side

Moody Jack-O'-Lanterns

Children grow and mature emotionally by facing openly their changing moods. Discussing their feelings with each other helps students to better understand themselves and other people. When children understand and accept their feelings, they are in a better position to manage their behavior. One of the most successful ways to have young children study their moods and emotions is through their own creative art work in which they are encouraged to express feelings.

Purposes and Objectives

1. To help children discuss their moods and emotions
2. To give them opportunities to express their feelings in art

Number of Participants

Any number

Materials Needed

- ☐ Manila paper
- ☐ Crayons or colored chalk
- ☐ Scissors
- ☐ Black felt-point pen

STUDENT DIRECTIONS

1. Draw a card from the box.

2. Read the situation on the card.

3. Think about how you would feel if it happened to you.

4. Make a large Jack-o'-lantern and let its face show how you feel.

5. Cut out the Jack-o'-lantern and paste it on black paper.

6. Place your picture on the bulletin board.

Instructions for Making Aid

Read aloud books that show intense, but completely normal, emotions. *Alexander and the Terrible, Horrible, No Good, Very Bad Day* by Judith Viorst, *To Hilda for Helping* by Margot Zemach, and *Noisy Nora* by Rosemary Wells are books that describe intense feelings. Follow the readings with discussions of the characters' attitudes and behavior.

Provide a box of cards containing brief vignettes or situations that elicit emotional responses from students. Ask them to depict their reactions to the situations in art form.

Situations such as those listed below may be used to generate discussion.

Your mother says "no" when you ask to spend the night with a friend.

You make an *A* on your math test.

A car runs over your new bicycle.

Your best friend moves to a distant city.

The dentist tells you that you have a cavity.

You are invited to a birthday party.

A big dog chases you down the street.

You are watching a horror movie on T.V.

You slam the car door on your finger.

Your television set is broken.

Variations and Teaching Hints

This project may be carried out at various times during the year by substituting valentines, snowmen, shamrocks, or other shapes for the Jack-o'-lanterns.

Moody Jack-o-Lanterns

Surprise

Happiness

Sadness

Fright

Evaluation

1. Improved discussion skills
2. Better understanding of human emotions
3. Evidence of improved self-discipline

Felt Books

Felt books are just what the name implies—pages of felt fastened together to form soft, quiet books of activities for young children. The books are designed to be used at the reading readiness level and are comprised mainly of manipulative rather than reading materials. A felt book is actually more like a toy than a book. It entertains children and gives them an opportunity to practice skills.

Because it is impossible for children to share materials without talking with each other, the felt book becomes a catalyst for language development when two young children work together.

Purposes and Objectives

1. To give practice in manipulative skills
2. To give practice in visual discrimination
3. To give practice in oral communication

Number of Participants

Two per book

Materials Needed

- □ Felt in assorted colors
- □ Pinking shears
- □ Scissors
- □ Black felt-point pen
- □ Collection of small pictures
- □ Scraps of yarn, ribbon, buttons, and other materials for trimming
- □ Shoestrings
- □ White glue

Instructions for Making Aid

With pinking shears, cut approximately twenty pieces of felt into 8 ½″ × 11″ pages. Sew or glue a pocket of felt to each left-hand page to hold manipulative materials, and plan an activity for each right-hand page (see illustration). The following are suggestions for activities.

1. A felt face with removable features and yarn hair to be braided
2. A felt shoe cutout with shoelace to be tied and untied
3. Geometric shapes cut from felt
4. Felt numerals and letters of the alphabet
5. Tic-tac-toe game played with felt dots
6. Buttons and buttonholes cut from an old shirt front
7. A zipper, snaps, and hooks and eyes to be opened and closed
8. A felt clock face with movable hands
9. Small pictures with felt backing for storytelling
10. A felt plate with knife, fork, spoon, and napkin

When an activity has been prepared for each page, punch holes in the pages and tie them together with a shoestring. Make as many felt books as time allows so that several pairs of children may work at one time.

Felt Book

Evaluation

1. Improvement in manipulative skills
2. Better visual discrimination
3. Ability to carry out a task independently

Milk Carton Puppets

No one knows for sure where or when the art of puppetry originated; but it is known that ancient burial grounds in all parts of the world have revealed small, carved figures, jointed in various ways to permit movement by hand.

Puppetry is widely used as an educational practice to dramatize events in history, to illustrate ways of life in other cultures, to encourage acceptable social behavior, to emphasize desirable health practices, to promote literature, and simply to stimulate oral language. In the hands of a child, a puppet becomes a tool for easier and more open expression.

One of the easiest papier-mâché puppets to make is one that has a cardboard milk carton as its base. This type of puppet is excellent for large audiences because it can be seen easily from a distance.

Purposes and Objectives

1. To provide a tool that stimulates speaking and listening skills
2. To promote literature through dramatization

Number of Participants

Any number

Materials Needed

- ☐ Several empty one-half gallon milk cartons
- ☐ Balloons
- ☐ Wheat paste (wallpaper paste)
- ☐ Newspapers
- ☐ Scissors
- ☐ Masking tape
- ☐ Tempera paint and cloth scraps for trimming puppets

Instructions for Making Aid

Cut the top from a milk carton and partially insert an inflated balloon into the opening. Secure the balloon with a strip of masking tape. Cover the balloon and the top portion of the carton with several layers of torn newspaper strips that have been dipped in paste. Allow the mâché to dry completely. When dry, the balloon should be deflated by inserting a straight pin; a strong structure will remain to be decorated with paint and scraps. Cut the bottom from the carton.

A drawstring slip cover should be made to form the clothing of a human character or the fur of an animal. The cover also conceals the arm of the puppeteer. A milk carton puppet is large and will require the length of a child's forearm to manipulate it.

STUDENT DIRECTIONS

1. Select a story for your puppet play.

2. Decorate puppets to match the characters.

3. Prepare the story as a script.

4. Assign parts and rehearse the script.

5. Perform the play for your classmates.

6. Take your play "on the road" to other classes.

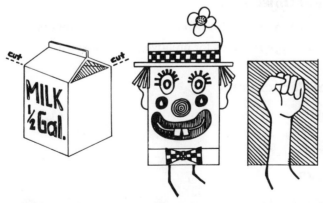

Milk Carton Puppets

Variations and Teaching Hints

For puppet plays, students should be assisted in finding stories with lively dialogue, much action, a conflict to be resolved, heroes that do things, a rousing climax, and a satisfying ending. Folk tales, of course, contain all these elements and are perfect for puppet plays. Some of the most popular stories used for puppet presentations are "Cinderella," "Rapunzel," "Rumpelstiltskin," "Mr. and Mrs. Vinegar," "The Bremen Town Musicians," and "Sleeping Beauty." A wide variety of contemporary stories are also suitable for puppetry.

Evaluation

1. Evidence of improved oral expression
2. Attentive listening on the part of the audience
3. Independence in carrying out a project

Puppet Stages

Most puppet shows are enhanced by the use of a stage. The main purpose of a puppet stage is to focus the attention of the audience on the puppets. The stage is made to block off areas the puppeteer does not want the audience to see. Problems of stage construction, backdrops for scenery, and modeling of puppet characters provide valuable opportunities for the development of creative thinking. We will briefly describe three stages easily constructed by children for classroom use.

Purpose and Objectives

1. To provide practice in following a sequence of directions
2. To provide opportunities for creative problem solving

Number of Participants

Small group

Materials Needed

CHAIR STAGE

- Two large chairs
- Heavy-duty dowel, broom, or mop handle
- Blanket, tablecloth, or sheet

DOORWAY STAGE

☐ Rope

☐ Blanket, tablecloth, or sheet

TABLE STAGE

☐ Classroom table

☐ Blanket, tablecloth, or sheet

STUDENT DIRECTIONS

A. Directions for making a chair stage:

1. Place two chairs about four feet from each other.

2. Secure a broom, dowel, or mop handle between the two chairs.

3. Place a blanket or tablecloth over the rod.

4. Arrange the stage so the audience can see the puppets.

B. Directions for making a doorway stage:

1. Place two chairs in the hall outside the door.

2. Fasten a piece of rope between the two chairs.

3. When the rope is secure, place a blanket, tablecloth, or sheet over the rope.

4. Adjust the rope and blanket so that the puppets will be clearly seen.

C. Directions for making a table stage:

1. Turn a classroom table on its side.

2. Place a blanket or cloth over the table top.

3. Place the table stage so that audience can easily see the puppets.

Variations and Teaching Hints

There are many other types of puppet stages suitable for the elementary class-room. For example, cardboard boxes of various shapes and sizes are frequently used as puppet theatres. The box must be large enough to allow freedom of movement for the puppeteers. After appropriate openings are cut in the box, the imaginative use of tempera paint transforms a shipping container into a creative dramatics center.

An *apron stage* is the most professional type of puppet stage. Such stages are ordinarily constructed from plywood in a three-part, folding-screen arrangement. It is important to make the apron stage portable and durable. Most books on puppetry give directions for constructing more complex types of stages.

Evaluation

1. Heightened student interest in puppetry
2. Improved proficiency in following a sequence of directions
3. Increased ability to understand problems and solve them creatively

Puppet Stages

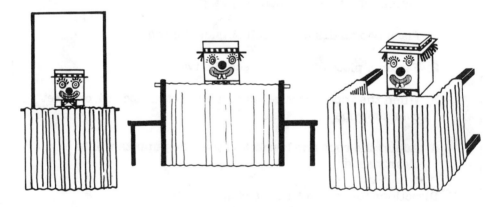

PART V

ACTIVITIES TO ENRICH LISTENING

Lucy the Listener

There are four main steps that must be emphasized if children are to develop the skill of efficient listening. First, they need to understand the significance of receiving both verbal and nonverbal signals in the act of communication. Next, they should become aware that reading, writing, speaking, and listening are interrelated. One depends on the others. Third, students must learn to evaluate their own ability to listen in an effective way. They should evaluate with an eye toward improvement. Finally, it is imperative that they hear many examples of the very best language used in the very best way. Reading aloud to them from excellent literature provides an opportunity to accomplish all four steps.

For this activity to have any lasting effect on classroom listening, you should prepare a list of listening criteria for your students to follow (see illustration). The list of standards should be reviewed before and after planned listening experiences. Students may then analyze their own listening behavior. A list of books recommended for reading aloud as examples of rich language usage is provided in Appendices N and O.

Purposes and Objectives

1. To help students interpret verbal and nonverbal signals for better understanding of language
2. To show students that reading, writing, speaking, and listening are related and interwoven.
3. To give students a means of evaluating their own listening abilities
4. To offer examples of rich and provocative oral language

Number of Participants

Any number

Materials Needed

- ☐ Chart of listening criteria
- ☐ Books for reading aloud

STUDENT DIRECTIONS

1. Study the Lucy the Listener chart.

2. Listen as your teacher reads a book.

3. Check yourself to see if you followed the directions on the chart.

4. Work to improve your listening habits.

Instructions for Making Aid

Enlarge the chart of listening standards shown in the illustration. A Lionel the Listener chart may be used if you prefer. Paint the chart in bright colors and post it at the children's eye level. Carefully review and discuss each standard on the list.

Prepare for reading books aloud according to the following guidelines:

1. Establish a regular schedule for reading aloud.
2. Choose books that your students are sure to enjoy.
3. Select books that you, too, will enjoy.
4. Practice reading the book aloud.
5. Create an atmosphere conducive to listening.
6. Eliminate undue distractions.
7. Read with feeling and expression.
8. Maintain as much eye contact as possible.
9. Use gestures and body language to help convey meaning.
10. Discuss unfamiliar words.
11. Point out the various parts of a book and call them by name.
12. Elicit responses to the story.

Lucy the Listener

1. Sits in a comfortable position
2. Looks at the speaker
3. Thinks about what is being said
4. Picks out the main idea
5. Listens for supporting facts
6. Takes advantage of body language
7. Thinks over what has been said
8. Evaluates what has been said

Variations and Teaching Hints

This mini-unit on listening should be taught early in the school year in order for its benefits to be reflected in classroom listening behavior. This activity may be repeated periodically throughout the year.

Evaluation

1. Evidence of improved listening behavior
2. Fewer errors and misconceptions caused by poor listening habits
3. A wider interest in language usage
4. Increasing ability to evaluate listening habits
5. An awareness of body language

Sound Bingo

Young children need a great deal of practice in identifying initial consonant sounds; therefore, variety in practice sessions becomes very important. Sound Bingo is an easy game to prepare and is simple and convenient for children to use. It provides an enjoyable means of reinforcing a phonics skill.

Purposes and Objectives

1. To give practice in identifying initial consonant sounds
2. To sharpen the ability to hear variations in sounds

Number of Participants

Four to six

Materials Needed

- ☐ White poster board
- ☐ Collection of small pictures (see illustration)
- ☐ Scissors
- ☐ Paste
- ☐ Black felt-point pen
- ☐ Clear contact paper
- ☐ Bottle tops

Instructions for Making Aid

Prepare at least six bingo cards by cutting and pasting twenty-five small pictures on cards to illustrate initial consonant sounds. The pictures should be arranged differently on each card, but in rows of five. Laminate the cards with clear contact paper.

Cut a cardboard circle and label it with eight different consonants. Make a spinner for the wheel.

When players are assembled, and cards and bottle tops are distributed, the game is played in the following manner:

1. The first player spins the spinner and calls out the letter indicated.
2. Each player places a marker (bottle top) on one picture that begins with the sound of the letter named.
3. The next player spins and the game continues.
4. The first player to place five tops in a row, either down or across, calls "Bingo" and is the winner.

Variations and Teaching Hints

Final consonants may be substituted for initial ones to add variety and to further strengthen listening skills.

Evaluation

1. Evidence of increased skill in hearing initial sounds
2. Awareness of subtle variations in sounds

Story Murals

Reading aloud to children from an interesting library book is one of the most effective ways to help them develop their listening skills. The activity may be further enhanced by having the students respond to the story with a related art experience.

Story murals are fun to make and fascinating to look at; but more important is the fact that they help to extend the students' comprehension of a story. The teacher's role is to prepare the story, read it well, and then to provide the materials for students to use in making a graphic response.

Purposes and Objectives

1. To improve the listening skills of students
2. To enrich a literature experience
3. To conduct a satisfying group project

Number of Participants

Any number

Materials Needed

- ☐ Book short enough to be read aloud at one sitting (see Appendix N)
- ☐ Wrapping paper, about five yards
- ☐ White or buff art paper
- ☐ Crayons or colored chalk
- ☐ Scissors
- ☐ Wheat paste and brushes
- ☐ Stick-on letters

Instructions for Making Aid

Arrange the wrapping paper—the background for the mural—on the bulletin board within reach of the children. Place the mixed paste and the brushes alongside. Have students paint shapes that represent the story and paste them on the background. Use stick-on letters to make a caption in keeping with the book. Read the story again as students enjoy their handiwork.

Variations and Teaching Hints

It is good, on occasion, for students to paint with tempera paint directly on the surface of the mural. A mural of this type takes longer because students are forced to take turns; however, the results are worth the added inconvenience.

Evaluation

1. More attentive listening to the reading of a book
2. Evidence of a greater appreciation for literature
3. Increasing maturity in cooperating on a group project

Canned Consonants

Beginning readers need a great deal of practice in recognizing initial consonant sounds, and a variety of exercises must be provided to minimize the risk of monotony and boredom. Canned Consonants is an activity designed to provide practice in a game format.

Purposes and Objectives

1. To reinforce initial consonant sounds
2. To create an awareness of and interest in word families or *phonograms*

Canned Consonants

Number of Participants

Two

Materials Needed

☐ Several empty cans with labels removed

☐ Heavy white paper

☐ Black felt-point pen

☐ Scissors

☐ Transparent tape

☐ List of phonograms (see Appendix C)

Instructions for Making Aid

Cut a piece of white paper to fit around the can. Cut a 2" band off the end of the piece. Tape both pieces around the can. Write consonants on the narrow band and the remainder of a phonogram on the wider band as shown in the illustration. When the bands of paper are rotated, a new word will be formed as each new consonant matches up with the ending. Two players take turns in rotating the paper and reading the words orally.

This game costs nothing and takes only a few minutes to make; thus it is a simple matter to make up one game for each word family to be learned (see Appendix C).

Display and Storage

The finished games may be stored in a large brown grocery bag labeled "Canned Consonants" and placed in the manipulative materials center for children to use as an independent activity.

Variations and Teaching Hints

When students have mastered the skill of identifying initial consonant sounds, this game becomes an excellent spelling acitivity. One student rotates the paper band and pronounces the word; the partner spells it orally.

Evaluation

1. Greater competency in recognizing initial consonant sounds

2. Wider use of phonograms as sight words

3. Greater accuracy in the spelling of phonograms in written work

Sound Barrels and Boxes

An effective way to give young children practice in distinguishing beginning consonant sounds is to have them classify pictures according to their initial sounds. Students can work at this activity independently if you write the appropriate letter on the back of each picture.

Purposes and Objectives

1. To give practice in beginning sounds
2. To provide an independent activity for children at the readiness and beginning reading levels.

Number of Participants

One to four

Materials Needed

☐ Corrugated cardboard 22″ × 28″

☐ Twenty-six paper cups

☐ Stick-on alphabet

☐ Twenty-six brads (paper fasteners)

Instructions for Making Aid

Use the paper fasteners to attach paper cups to the corrugated cardboard. Label each cup with a letter of the alphabet (see illustration). Fill each paper cup with small pictures representing each letter. For self-checking, the correct letter should be printed on the back of each picture.

For practice in beginning sounds, have students take out the pictures, spread them on the floor or tabletop, say the name of each picture, and reclassify it according to beginning sound. When all sounds have been sorted into the cups, children may check for accuracy by looking on the back of each picture.

Variations and Teaching Hints

A variation on this activity is to fill boxes, cartons, or cans with small objects instead of pictures, which are then classified by beginning sounds. A soft drink case with twenty-four compartments also works well for these activities if each box is labeled with a letter of the alphabet (combine *W* with *X* and *Y* with *Z*.)

Evaluation

1. Increased awareness of initial sounds
2. Greater efficiency in classifying

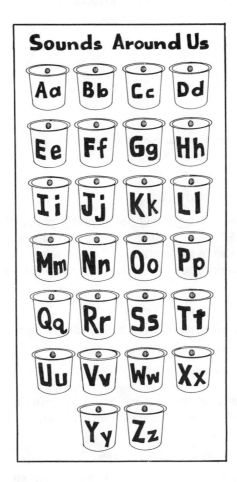

Memory Mandala

The mandala, a graphic image in the form of a circle, is a very old artistic symbol representing the universe. In oriental countries, it is painted on silk, paper, wood, and other materials, in beautiful patterns.

In the primary classroom, creating a mandala is a useful aid for improving the listening habits of children and is also a satisfying art activity.

Purposes and Objectives

1. To encourage students to listen carefully to oral directions and to remember them long enough to carry out a task
2. To provide a convenient means of evaluating the ability to follow oral directions

Number of Participants

Any number

Materials Needed

☐ White mimeograph paper (two pages per student)
☐ Crayons

Instructions for Making Aid

Cut a large circle from each page of mimeograph paper. Give each student two circles. Ask them to fold each circle in half and then into fourths. Have them mark on the fold lines to divide the sections. When all students are ready, read them the directions for decorating each section. Use simple, clear-cut directions such as the following:

1. In one section, make six red squares.
2. In one section, make three green trees with black trunks.
3. In one section, make eight orange balls.
4. In one section, make six red balloons.

When the students have finished one mandala, have them check their work as you reread the directions. Proceed to the second design with directions such as the following:

1. In one section, draw six yellow rabbits.
2. In one section, draw three red flowers with green stems.
3. In one section, draw three green houses with red roofs.
4. In one section, draw four snowmen with black top hats.

Again, have students' check their work as you reread the directions.

Display

Staple each student's mandalas together, back to back, and hang them as mobiles from a piece of string.

Variations and Teaching Hints

Directions for decorating the mandalas may be simplified or made more challenging to fit the developmental level of different groups of children.

By using a new set of directions, you can repeat the activity every few weeks and observe the students' progress. Use colored markers or colored chalk for variety and display the mandalas in different ways.

Evaluation

1. Evidence of greater accuracy in following oral directions
2. Ability to devote sustained attention to an intricate task

Memory Mandala

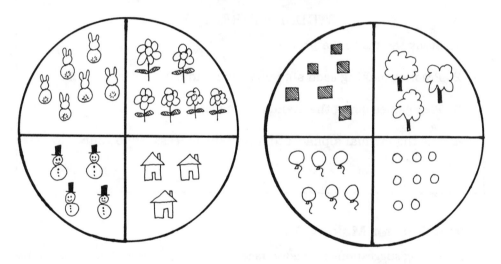

Manual Alphabet

Students who have no hearing loss may learn to communicate with a hearing-impaired student by using the manual alphabet to spell words in a message. If students are provided a copy of the alphabet and several activities to give them practice in using it, they quickly learn the gestures and make use of them on many occasions to talk with friends in and out of the classroom.

Purposes and Objectives

1. To create a better understanding between students who have hearing loss and those who do not

2. To give hearing students a new and silent means of communication

Number of Participants

Any number

Materials Needed

☐ Copies of the manual alphabet for each student and several copies to cut up for games (see illustration)

STUDENT DIRECTIONS

1. Study the manual alphabet.

2. Practice making each sign until you know the entire alphabet.

3. Play games using the manual alphabet.

4. Use the manual alphabet to finger spell messages to your friends.

Instructions for Making Aid

The following suggestions take advantage of other activities and materials in this book to give practice on the manual alphabet and numerals.

1. Use the sound barrels described on page 161, and paste a small picture (cut from the manual alphabet) on each cup in alphabetical order. Follow directions for using the sound barrels.

2. Use the sentence building blocks described on page 115, and paste letters from the manual alphabet together to spell the words indicated. Follow directions for the sentence building blocks activity.

3. Follow directions for the holiday vocabulary chart on page 113, and paste letters from the manual alphabet to spell the word beside each picture.

4. Allow students to work at the multi-purpose board, described on page 97, to match manual numeral signs with their corresponding number symbols.

5. Paste individual letters from the manual alphabet on strips to be used in the seasonal T-scopes shown on page 13.

6. Make cards similar to those used in the bleach bottle T-scope shown on page 15, and substitute words spelled with the manual alphabet for those at the top of each card.

Variations and Teaching Hints

Use of the manual alphabet should, of course, be optional for hearing students. If it is made available in the regular classroom, however, most students will choose to learn it. They see at once the value of knowing and using such a tool.

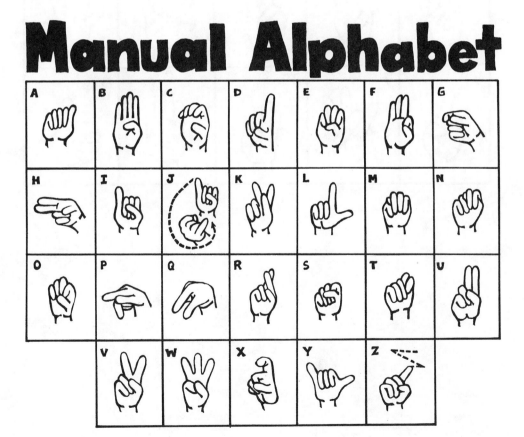

Evaluation

1. Evidence of better communication between hearing students and those with a hearing loss
2. Awareness of a new means of communication
3. Greater attentiveness toward others who are attempting to communicate

Manual Numerals

PART VI

ACTIVITIES TO ENRICH LITERATURE AND LIBRARY PROGRAMS

Reading Record Chart

The value of a child's own personal reading record has been discovered by many teachers. A graphic record of accomplishment is extremely important because it helps to satisfy a child's need for recognition of achievement and encourages sustained silent reading. Such a record is more significant to the student than a record kept by the teacher, simply because the child becomes responsible for the activities necessary in keeping the record. Positive reinforcement is gained each time an addition is made in the record.

The reading record chart is made by attaching a series of pockets to poster board, plywood, or a bulletin board. When names or numbers are fastened to the pockets, they become personal storage spaces for book cards. As each library book is completed, the student writes its title, author, and the date on a small card and files it in his or her special pocket. Enjoyment comes first in reading the book and secondly in watching the card pack grow.

Some criteria helpful to the teacher in constructing a reading record chart are the following:

1. The chart should be attractive. Because it will remain in view over long periods of time, it should also be used as a beauty spot in the classroom.

2. The chart should contain a caption that promotes books and reading. Famous quotations on books and reading from Bartlett's *Familiar Quotations* are excellent for captions and may also provide a theme for the chart (see Appendix P).

3. The chart should be durable. Because it is posted at eye level and is in constant use by children, it must be well constructed of sturdy materials.

4. The chart should be noncompetitive. Each pocket should be considered private property and no comparisons are made. The only competition should be the child's own past record. Because reading the books and keeping the record are sufficiently pleasurable, tangible rewards are not necessary.

5. The chart should be expandable. Extra pockets need to be prepared in advance so that newcomers to the class can participate in the project without delay.

Purposes and Objectives

1. To stimulate wider reading in self-selected library books
2. To show independent reading progress to students and parents

Number of Participants

Any number

STUDENT DIRECTIONS

1. Read a library book of your choice.

2. Write the title, author, and the date on a 3" × 5" card.

3. Put the card in your chart pocket.

4. Read another book and add a card.

5. Count your cards at the end of each month.

Materials Needed

- ☐ Poster paper: two dark blue, one red, one white
- ☐ Brads (paper fasteners)
- ☐ Stick-on letters or black felt-point pen for hand lettering
- ☐ Stick-on numerals
- ☐ 3" × 5" index cards
- ☐ White glue

Reading Record Chart

Cut out this area

To the back, apply a square of black paper glued around the edges to form a pocket.

Instructions for Making Aid

Splice two pages of blue poster board together to form a chart 28" × 44" in size. Cut red boats and white sails according to the pattern on page 170. Make one boat and sail for each student in the class. Glue white sails to the background. Use paper fasteners to attach boats, leaving the boat open to receive cards. Attach a caption to the top of the chart. Place blank index cards near the chart.

Variations and Teaching Hints

For economy and convenience, the index cards may be cut in half lengthwise. When a pocket is full, the reader may take the cards home for parents to see or they may be filed in a folder until the end of the semester. This project will be much more successful if the classroom library collection contains an ample number of multiethnic and easy-to-read books. For older students the chart may be made more sophisticated by using plain pockets.

As to the efficacy of the reading record chart, teachers will at once recognize it as a motivational device to be abandoned when a child no longer needs it or to be omitted altogether for the child who reads widely but has no interest in keeping a record.

An important concomitant value of the students' reading record is its use in parent-teacher conferences to illustrate the child's reading level and interests, and the amount of reading taking place.

Evaluation

1. Wider reading of self-selected library books
2. Improvement in comprehension skills
3. Greater interest in silent reading

Dial-a-Book

Many students who are able to read well still fail to read a wide variety of literature. They need to be directed into areas they tend to neglect, such as travel, poetry, and drama.

Dial-a-Book is an activity that introduces an element of chance and risk into book selection and thus captures the imagination of students. They simply spin the number wheel and commit themselves to read a book in the category indicated. Over a period of time, their reading will automatically include many types of literature.

Purposes and Objectives

1. To encourage students to include many types of literature in their reading
2. To add an element of adventure to book selection

Number of Participants

Any number

Materials Needed

☐ Corrugated cardboard or thin plywood

☐ Spinner made from cardboard or wood

☐ Stick-on numerals or felt-point pen for hand lettering

☐ Poster containing a caption and a list of book categories

Instructions for Making Aid

Construct a chart similar to the one in the illustration. List the categories of literature suitable for the grade level under consideration. Number the categories from *1* through *12*. Keep in mind that students very much enjoy having some *free choices*.

Construct a spinner wheel by cutting a large circle from cardboard or plywood. Divide the wheel into twelve sections and number each one. Attach the spinner. Check to make certain that it spins freely. Place the spinner near the chart.

STUDENT DIRECTIONS

1. Spin the wheel and let the spinner come to a complete stop.

2. Go to the library center and select a book from the category indicated.

3. Read your book and record it on your record chart.

Variations and Teaching Hints

Some students may not need to use a motivational aid in order to read widely. Of course, those students should not use this activity. It should however, be available and optional to all students in a class who wish to use it.

Dial-a-Book is more effective as an activity if a progress chart such as the one on page 175 is used in conjunction with it.

Evaluation

1. Wider reading in all types of literature
2. Evidence of a growing maturity in book selection
3. Greater enthusiasm for independent reading

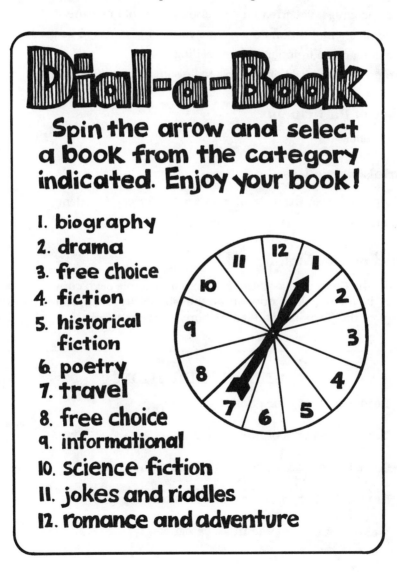

Dial-a-Book

Spin the arrow and select a book from the category indicated. Enjoy your book!

1. biography
2. drama
3. free choice
4. fiction
5. historical fiction
6. poetry
7. travel
8. free choice
9. informational
10. science fiction
11. jokes and riddles
12. romance and adventure

Colorful Classifications

Students and their parents benefit from seeing graphic proof of progress in all areas. Most people would find themselves reading more books and in greater variety if they kept a running record of their reading. This acitvity is designed to provide reading records for upper elementary students.

Purposes and Objectives

1. To encourage wider reading in various types of literature
2. To provide motivation for a greater number of books to be read
3. To add appeal to independent reading
4. To provide a record of progress to be sent to parents

Number of Participants

Any number

Materials Needed

☐   Copy of the record or graph on page 175 for each student

☐   Colored markers or map pencils

Instructions for Making Aid

Duplicate the Colorful Classifications chart and staple each copy inside a manila folder. Write the names of students on the tabs. Distribute the folders to students and explain the purposes and instructions for using them.

STUDENT DIRECTIONS

1. Read a book of your choice.

2. Decide what type of literature it is.

3. Color in a square (a "book") on the right shelf.

4. Use a different color for each literature type.

5. Make an effort to read in all categories.

Colorful Classifications

biography | 1 2 3 4 5 6 7 8 9 10

drama | 1 2 3 4 5 6 7 8 9 10

fiction | 1 2 3 4 5 6 7 8 9 10

historical fiction | 1 2 3 4 5 6 7 8 9 10

informational | 1 2 3 4 5 6 7 8 9 10

jokes and riddles | 1 2 3 4 5 6 7 8 9 10

romance and adventure | 1 2 3 4 5 6 7 8 9 10

poetry | 1 2 3 4 5 6 7 8 9 10

travel | 1 2 3 4 5 6 7 8 9 10

science fiction | 1 2 3 4 5 6 7 8 9 10

Variations and Teaching Hints

Students should be commended for efforts in reading widely whether or not they reach the goal of one hundred books. Encourage students to keep the record for more than one year.

Evaluation

1. Increase in the amount of independent, self-selected reading
2. Evidence of widening interests in reading

Dewey Decimal Scavenger Hunt

Melvil Dewey, probably more than any other single individual, was responsible for the development of library science in the United States. Most people, however, know him as the originator of the Dewey decimal system, a method of classifying all books. In the Dewey decimal system, books are numerically arranged on the shelf; thus, anyone who can count and knows the number of the book can find it easily. Children should learn about all call numbers because virtually every elementary school library classifies its books according to Dewey's system (see illustration). Students should also be familiar with fiction and nonfiction books, reference books, and biographies.

Purposes and Objectives

1. To help students learn to locate books in the elementary school library
2. To reinforce student understanding of the Dewey decimal system

Number of Participants

Four to ten

Materials Needed

- ☐ Strips of construction paper in thirteen different colors
- ☐ Felt-tip markers
- ☐ Cardboard

Instructions for Making Aid

1. Develop book lists, one for each team of two players, using the following format:

TITLE	AUTHOR	CALL NUMBER
World Book, Vol I	Lewallen	000
You and Your Amazing Mind	Maxwell	150
The Bible Story	Sechrist	220.9
Christmas Everywhere	Waller	400
Our American Language	Raymond	568
Album of Horses	Henry	636
Joe Namath	Olsen	796
Zoo: A Book of Poems	Hopkins	811
Indians	Tunis	970.1
Justin Morgan Had a Horse	Henry	F
Frederick	Lionni	E
Abraham Lincoln	D'Aulaire	B

2. Scramble the sequence of the books so that all lists have a different order.
3. Label the strips "000," "200," and so forth. If the book is 394.2, it should have five strips (or one strip for each team) with "394.2" written on them.
4. Place a different set of colored strips in each book on the list. For example, if you have five teams, five strips should be placed in each book.
5. Repeat the process for each of the books.
6. Place the books in the correct space on the shelf before the game begins.

Variations and Teaching Hints

Many variations of the basic game might be developed. For example, the teacher could present different lists to each group. This would mean that each team would be looking for different books. Another alternative is to omit some of the basic information on the book list, that is, the call number, title, or author (omit only one piece of information, however). Another variation would require the teams to seek some of the needed information from the card catalog or some other source. Place a Dewey decimal system chart in a prominent location in the library before beginning the game.

Evaluation

1. Success in locating various books in the elementary school library
2. Understanding of the Dewey decimal system
3. Ability to apply the Dewey decimal system of classification

THE DEWEY DECIMAL SYSTEM

WHO AM I?
100-199

WHO MADE ME?
200-299

WHO IS THE MAN IN THE NEXT CAVE?   300-399

HOW CAN I MAKE THAT MAN UNDERSTAND ME?
400-499

WHAT MAKES THINGS HAPPEN IN THE WORLD AROUND ME? 500-599

HOW CAN I CONTROL NATURE?
600-699

HOW CAN I ENJOY MY SPARE TIME?   700-799

WHAT ARE THE STORIES OF MAN'S GREAT THOUGHTS AND DEEDS?
800-899

HOW CAN I RECORD WHAT MAN HAS DONE?
900-999

HOW CAN I STORE FACTS IN BOOKS?

000-099

STUDENT DIRECTIONS

1. Select a partner for the Dewey Decimal Scavenger Hunt.

2. Take a book list from the box.

3. Find each of the books on the list in the correct sequence.

4. When you locate a book, take one colored marker f .r your team.

5. Put the book back in its proper place on the shelf.

6. Find the next book on the list.

7. The winner is the first team to locate all the books on the list.

8. Return all the book slips to the teacher.

Card Catalog Clue

Libraries play an essential role in the language arts program. As a result, most schools emphasize the role of the classroom teacher in encouraging student growth in library skills by means of systematic instruction and constant reinforcement. A board game may be developed to promote student understanding of reference books, the arrangement of the library, and the card catalog.

Purposes and Objectives

1. To guide practice in locating various types of books found in the card catalog

2. To reinforce student understanding of the terms fiction and nonfiction

3. To offer practice in recognizing the numerical arrangement of the Dewey decimal system

Number of Participants

Two to four

Materials Needed

☐ Poster board or oaktag, 20" × 20"

☐ Colored marking pens

☐ Game tokens (beans, buttons)

☐ Die

☐ Markers in the denomination of five, ten, and twenty points

---

STUDENT DIRECTIONS

1. Place your marker on the "go" space.

2. Roll the die, and move the appropriate number of spaces.

3. Decide if the square refers to a fiction or nonfiction book. If you are wrong, your turn is over. If you are correct, take a card from the appropriate pile and answer the question. Check your answer by looking on the reverse side of the card.

4. If you are correct, take five points from the bank. You receive no points for an incorrect answer.

5. The next player takes a turn.

6. The player who passes the card catalog receives ten points. The player who lands on the card catalog, receives twenty points.

7. The game ends after a set length of time.

8. The player with the most points is the winner.

Instructions for Making Aid

1. Create a game board (see illustration).
2. Provide four game tokens.
3. Illustrate the game board with interesting pictures related to the library.

4. On the game board draw a card catalog like the one in your school library.

5. Develop fiction, nonfiction, and chance cards. The questions are on one side and the answers on the back.

Variations and Teaching Hints

Make up questions related to your own card catalog and book collection. The cards should be changed periodically or several versions of the game board prepared by changing the call numbers listed on the various squares. Other interesting variations may be introduced by producing cards of different levels of difficulty or with different point values.

Display and Storage

Provide a prominent place for the game whenever the topic of locational skills arises. For added durability, the board, tokens, and game cards should be laminated and placed in a decorated box.

Card Catalog Clue

A-Am 1.	Cn-Cz 6.	Fo-Fz 11.	J 16.	O 21.	Sr-Sz 26.
An-Az 2.	D-Do 7.	G 12.	K-L 17.	P 22.	T 27.
B-Be 3.	Dp-Dz 8.	H-Hi 13.	M-Me 18.	Q-R 23.	U 28.
Bi-Bz 4.	E 9.	Hj-Hz 14.	Mi-Mz 19.	S-Se 24.	V-W 29.
C-Cl 5.	F-Fl 10.	I 15.	N 20.	Sh-Sq 25.	X-Y-Z 30.

Evaluation

1. Increased proficiency in locating books in the library
2. Competence as determined by a worksheet on various elements found in the card catalog
3. Interest in the game

"Stained Glass" Book Reports

Sharing about what they read is one of the most successful ways for students to respond to literature. Book sharing also presents an excellent opportunity for them to recommend books to their peers. In planning book-sharing activities for students, art should play a prominent part. A satisfying aesthetic experience related to a book tends to make that book unforgettable.

Purposes and Objectives

1. To encourage students to respond to the books they read
2. To promote wide reading of library books
3. To give students a creative art experience

Number of Participants

Any number

Materials Needed

☐ Colored tissue paper
☐ White mimeograph paper
☐ Black construction paper
☐ Liquid starch
☐ Paint brushes
☐ Scissors

Instructions for Making Aid

Ask students to sketch, on a page of mimeograph paper, a scene or figure from a library book they have read. They should then fill in the spaces, in mosaic fashion, with small cut pieces of colored tissue paper pasted on with a brush dipped in liquid starch. Show the students how to fold a page of black construction paper and cut it to form a frame for the mosaic. When light shines through the tissue paper design, the artwork has the appearance of stained glass in a lead frame.

STUDENT DIRECTIONS

1. Think of an image that illustrates a library book you have read.

2. Draw the image on white paper.

3. Paste small pieces of colored tissue on the design.

4. Use black paper to cut a frame for your design.

5. Tape your "stained glass" picture on a window.

6. Describe the book scene to your friends.

"Stained Glass" Book Reports

1.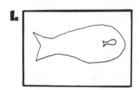

On heavy tracing or other translucent paper, draw basic pattern shapes.

2.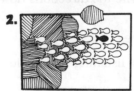

Glue cut or torn colored tissue pieces to cover surface of drawing.

3.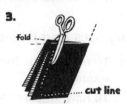

fold

····· cut line

Fold black paper as shown and cut outer border.

4.

Swimmy by Leo Leonni

Cut straight or curved strips to form "leading" lines.

Assemble strips and border and glue to picture.

Variations and Teaching Hints

One hundred alternatives to formal, written book reports are listed in Appendix Q.

Evaluation

1. Interest in depicting book scenes in art form
2. Increased discussion about self-selected reading

Student-Made Slides

The ability to follow directions is obviously a very important skill. It not only relates to the language arts, but also corresponds to many other activities both in and out of school. Students fail to comply with directions for a variety of reasons: The directions are poorly given, they are given over and over, or students hope someone else will follow the directions. Student-made slides is a how-to activity that requires students to follow a sequence of directions given orally by the teacher.

Give the students one direction at a time. When they have completed one direction, give them two directions to be followed in sequential order. After they have mastered two directions, give the students three, four, or five. Students should be encouraged to write the directions down when necessary.

Purposes and Objectives

1. To develop the habit of listening to directions in a chronological sequence
2. To have students follow multiple directions given by the teacher

Number of Participants

Small group

Materials Needed

☐ Small pictures printed on glossy stock
☐ Scissors
☐ Penny or other coin
☐ Clear contact paper

☐ Soapy water and paper towels

☐ Plastic slide mounts (2" × 2")

☐ Slide projector

☐ Hair spray or fixative

STUDENT DIRECTIONS

1. Cut pictures from glossy or high quality paper to a size of 2" × 2" (or smaller).

2. Cut a piece of clear contact paper approximately 2" × 2."

3. Peel off the paper backing from the plastic.

4. Place the plastic facedown.

5. Secure the picture to the sticky side of the plastic.

6. Rub a coin over the picture to remove any air bubbles.

7. Soak the picture in soapy water for two minutes.

8. Remove the picture from the water and shake off excess water.

9. Peel the paper from the plastic.

10. The picture should now appear on the plastic. Let it dry completely on a paper towel.

11. Carefully mount the picture in a 2" × 2" slide mount.

12. Snap the slide mount to close it.

13. Spray the slide with hair spray or fixative.

14. Place the slide in a projector for viewing.

15. Repeat the process to make a slide collection.

Instructions for Making Aid

1. Gather necessary materials.
2. Cluster students at tables or at desks pushed together.
3. Read the directions *twice.*
4. Answer any questions.
5. Distribute materials to student groups.

Note: Steps 3, 4, and 5 may be interchanged.

Variations and Teaching Hints

Making slides is only one activity to help students follow a sequence of directions. The projects should increase in difficulty; others might include the following:

- ☐ Paper hats
- ☐ Pinwheels
- ☐ Paper valentines
- ☐ Paper boats
- ☐ Cut-paper snowflakes
- ☐ Paper airplanes
- ☐ Fans
- ☐ Paper trees

Student-Made Slides

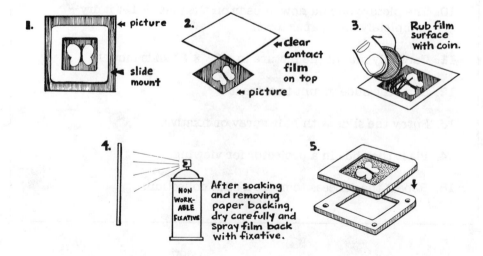

Display and Storage

Students could display their individual slides in a learning center along with the directions for viewing. The slides could become part of a narrated slide presentation produced by the students themselves.

Evaluation

1. Success in producing a slide
2. Increased ability to follow directions as they are presented
3. Improved ability in listening to oral directions

Caldecott Bingo

Several awards have been established to provide recognition for outstanding achievement in children's literature. The two most coveted awards in the United States, the Newbery medal and the Caldecott Medal, were established by Frederick G. Melcher, an American publisher. Both awards are administered by the American Library Association.

The Randolf Caldecott Medal is named in honor of a nineteenth century English illustrator. The Caldecott Medal, which was first awarded in 1938, is given to the illustrator of the most distinguished American picture book for children published during the previous year. Caldecott books help children to develop their artistic imagination and to become acquainted with people, experiences, and ideas in exciting ways. Games such as Caldecott Bingo can stimulate children to sample the Caldecott treasury (see Appendix R).

Purposes and Objectives

1. To encourage students to read Caldecott books and to savour the rich illustrations found in them
2. To develop an appreciation for the aesthetic features of a book

Number of Participants

Small to large group

Materials Needed

- Cardboard or poster board
- Individual sets of numbered markers
- Envelopes

Instructions for Making Aid

1. Cut a sufficient number of 10" × 12" cards for the entire class.
2. Grid the cards into a 5 × 5 pattern with 2" squares (see illustration).
3. Randomly write the names of twenty-five Caldecott Award books into the squares. No two cards should be the same.
4. Cut out 2" × 2" game tokens so students can cover their squares. Number the tokens from one to forty-four. There should be one set for each player.
5. Place the sets of tokens in individual student envelopes.

STUDENT DIRECTIONS

1. Place one Caldecott Bingo game card and one envelope containing game tokens on your desk.

2. Organize the tokens in numerical order. (If you are missing any of the tokens, tell the teacher.)

3. The teacher will call the number representing a Caldecott book and will give the *hard* clue.

4. If you know the book, place the appropriate token over the title on your card.

5. After the hard clues for all the titles have been exhausted, the *less difficult* clues will be called, and then the *author* clues.

6. "Bingo" is called by the first student to cover five titles in a row either down or across.

7. The teacher will then match the token numbers with the titles to see if you are correct.

Variations and Teaching Hints

The game could be simplified to include only twenty-five of the Caldecott books. Students could know which twenty-five were to be used in playing the game. Other variations might include using names of authors or illustrators. Reading selections other than Caldecott books might also be used. Bookmarks or other small prizes may be awarded.

Storage

The game cards and tokens are stored away until you are ready to use them with students or placed in a game center for student selection.

Evaluation

1. Recognition of the titles of books
2. Heightened interest in Caldecott Medal books
3. Wider reading of the award-winning books

CLUES FOR CALDECOTT BINGO

1. This was the first book to win the Caldecott award.
2. This is a collection of religious stories.
3. Dorothy Lathrop received the 1938 Caldecott Award for this book.

1. (*Animals of the Bible*)

1. This is a story of a New Year's Day celebration in China.
2. At midnight, the Kitchen God appeared behind the honey cakes that Mrs. Wang had cooked.
3. Thomas Handforth received the 1939 Caldecott Award for this book.

2. (*Mei Li*)

1. This book is the only biography on the Caldecott list.
2. This is a realistic account of one of America's most beloved heroes.
3. Ingri d'Aulaire and Edgar Parin d'Aulaire received the 1940 Caldecott Award for this book.

3. (*Abraham Lincoln*)

1. This is the story of the author's mother and father and of their mothers and fathers.
2. This is a story of a family tree.
3. Robert Lawson received the 1941 Caldecott Award for this book.

4. (*They Were Strong and Good*)

1. This story has its setting in the city of Boston.
2. A kindly policeman holds back the traffic for a family.
3. Robert McCloskey received the 1942 Caldecott Award for this book.

5. (*Make Way for Ducklings*)

1. This is a book that shows the four seasons of the year.
2. This story shows the unhappy results of too much progress.

3. Virginia Lee Burton received the 1943 Caldecott Award for this book.

6. (*The Little House*)

1. "Once upon a time, there lived a little Princess named Lenore" is the opening of this book.
2. This is a humorous story about a Royal Mathematician, a Court Jester, and a Royal Wizard.
3. Louis Slobodkin received the 1944 Caldecott Award for this book.

7. (*Many Moons*)

1. This is a religious book illustrated in muted, pastel colors.
2. This religious book is written in a poetic style for very young children.
3. Elizabeth Orton Jones received the 1945 Caldecott Award for this book.

8. (*Prayer for a Child*)

1. This book is a collection of American rhymes and jingles.
2. This book contains the folksong "Yankee Doodle."
3. Maud Petersham and Miska Petersham received the 1946 Caldecott Award for this book.

9. (*The Rooster Crows*)

1. In this story the fish tells the kitten that all land is one land.
2. This book tells how one part of the world depends on the other.
3. Leonard Weisgard received the 1947 Caldecott Award for this book.

10. (*The Little Island*)

1. This is a story about how parents, community helpers, and children carry out responsibility in a crisis.
2. This is a snow story that shows the first robin of spring.
3. Roger Duvoisin received the 1948 Caldecott Award for this book.

11. (*White Snow, Bright Snow*)

1. This is a realistic story of animal survival.
2. This is a tale of animal behavior.
3. Elmer Hader and Berta Hader received the 1949 Caldecott Award for this book.

12. (*The Big Snow*)

1. This is the story of Juan and the small village of Capistrano.
2. In this story, St. Joseph's Day is a special day at the Mission.

3. Leo Politi received the 1950 Caldecott Award for this book.

13. (Song of the Swallows)

1. This is a story of Pennsylvania Dutch art.
2. In this book, Grandmom painted the horn-blowing rooster.
3. Katherine Milhous received the 1951 Caldecott Award for this book.

14. (The Egg Tree)

1. In this story, an apprentice barber gives a haircut.
2. The plot is developed around an argument over food.
3. William Lipkind and Nicolas Mordvinoff received the 1952 Caldecott Award for this book.

15. (Finders Keepers)

1. In this book, Johnny's pet especially liked the maple sugar he brought from the store.
2. In the end, Johnny's pet finds a home in the zoo.
3. Lynd Ward received the 1953 Caldecott Award for this book.

16. (The Biggest Bear)

1. This story is a humorous tale about life in a convent.
2. French life on the streets of Paris is the setting for this dog story.
3. Ludwig Bemelmans received the 1954 Caldecott Award for this book.

17. (Madeline's Rescue)

1. This book is the French version of the world's best known folk tale.
2. There are more than three hundred versions of this rags to riches story.
3. Marcia Brown received the 1955 Caldecott Award for this book.

18. (Cinderella)

1. This book is a folk song about a wedding breakfast.
2. Mistress Mouse, Uncle Rat, and Mr. Cook all attend the celebration.
3. Feodor Rojankovsky received the 1956 Caldecott Award for this book.

19. (Frog Went A- Courtin')

1. In this story, "The cows lie down in the shade when it is hot."
2. This picture book about ecology emphasizes the need to protect growing things.
3. Marc Simont received the 1957 Caldecott Award for this book.

20. (A Tree Is Nice)

1. This book contains watercolor paintings of a hurricane.
2. The setting of this story is the seacoast of Maine.
3. Robert McCloskey received the 1958 Caldecott Award for this book.

21. (*Time of Wonder*)

1. This story was adapted from the *Canterbury Tales*.
2. This book is about a character who cannot resist flattery and almost loses his life.
3. Barbara Cooney received the 1959 Caldecott Award for this book.

22. (*Chanticleer and the Fox*)

1. This is the story of a piñata.
2. The heroine in this story is a Mexican girl named Ceci.
3. Marie Hall Ets received the 1960 Caldecott Award for this book.

23. (*Nine Days to Christmas*)

1. This story is a Russian Christmas legend.
2. This is a foreign version of our Santa Claus legend.
3. Nicholas Sidjakov received the 1961 Caldecott Award for this book.

24. (*Baboushka and the Three Kings*)

1. This book tells a fable from India and is illustrated in wood-block prints.
2. In this tale an old hermit has magical powers.
3. Marcia Brown received the 1962 Caldecott Award for this book.

25. (*Once a Mouse*)

1. In this story a small boy named Peter is the hero.
2. This is the first book in a series of stories about Peter.
3. Ezra Jack Keats received the 1963 Caldecott Award for this book.

26. (*The Snowy Day*)

1. This is a story in which food is withheld as punishment.
2. This is a controversial book that pictures monsters.
3. Maurice Sendak received the 1964 Caldecott Award for this book.

27. (*Where the Wild Things Are*)

1. This is an accumulative story about zoo animals.
2. Written in verse, this story presents the days of the week.
3. Beni Montresor received the 1965 Caldecott Award for this book.

28. (*May I Bring a Friend?*)

1. This story is a ballad written in Scottish dialect.
2. This book contains a glossary of Scottish words.
3. Nonny Hogrogian received the 1966 Caldecott Award for this book.

29. (*Always Room for One More*)

1. In this book a young girl creates stories based on her daydreams.
2. A surprise ending in this story features a kangaroo rat.
3. Evaline Ness received the 1967 Caldecott Award for this book.

30. (*Sam, Bangs and Moonshine*)

1. This is a story that ends with a loud "Kahbahbloom."
2. A military theme in red, white, and blue is illustrated in this book.
3. Ed Emberley received the 1968 Caldecott Award for this book.

31. (*Drummer Hoff*)

1. This is a Russian folk tale about a young man who seeks his fortune and marries the Czar's daughter.
2. This book is a Russian "noodle" story.
3. Uri Schulevitz received the 1969 Caldecott Award for this book.

32. (*The Fool of the World and the Flying Ship*)

1. This story is written and illustrated by a famous cartoonist.
2. A magic pebble saves the hero of this book.
3. William Steig received the 1970 Caldecott Award for this book.

33. (*Sylvester and the Magic Pebble*)

1. An African storyteller's style gave this book its title.
2. This is a legend about how folk tales came to be.
3. Gail E. Haley received the 1971 Caldecott Award for this book.

34. (*A Story—A Story*)

1. This is the story about a fox who wants his tail back.
2. After meeting a cow, a fair maiden, a peddler, and a hen, the fox wins back his tail.
3. Nonny Hogrogian received the 1972 Caldecott Award for this book.

35. (*One Fine Day*)

1. This is a Japanese folk tale about a woman who laughs at the wicked Oni.
2. She has a magic paddle that makes a potful of rice from one grain.

3. Blair Lent received the 1973 Caldecott Award for this book.

36. (The Funny Little Woman)

1. This story is the Cornish version of Rumpelstiltskin.
2. In this story the spinning is done by a squinny-eyed creature with a long tail.
3. Margot Zemach received the 1974 Caldecott Award for this book.

37. (Duffy and the Devil)

1. This book is a Pueblo Indian tale that is illustrated in vibrant colors.
2. A Pueblo Indian boy shoots arrows that link together to form a ladder.
3. Gerald McDermott received the 1975 Caldecott Award for this book.

38. (Arrow to the Sun)

1. An African folk tale about an iguana, a monkey, and Mother Owl.
2. One animal in this story has a guilty conscience and goes about whining.
3. Leo Dillon and Diane Dillon received the 1976 Caldecott Award for this book.

39. (Why Mosquitoes Buzz in People's Ears)

1. This is an African alphabet book.
2. This book is illustrated with pictures of the customs, traditions, people, plants, and animals of Africa.
3. Leo Dillon and Diane Dillon received the 1977 Caldecott Award for this book.

40. (Ashanti to Zulu: African Traditions)

1. This book is a Bible story told without words.
2. The time of the story lasts forty days and forty nights.
3. Peter Spier received the 1978 Caldecott Award for this book.

41. (Noah's Ark)

1. This is the story of an Indian girl who becomes a legend.
2. A raging storm shatters the girls' dream.
3. Paul Goble received the 1979 Caldecott Award for this book.

42. (The Girl Who Loved Wild Horses)

1. This is the story of a farmer who travels over hills, through valleys, by streams, past farms, and villages to sell his goods.
2. When the man's pockets are full of coins, he wanders through the market, buying provisions for his family.

3. Barbara Cooney received the 1980 Caldecott Award for this book.

43. (*Ox-Cart Man*)

1. This book shows a bear wearing a frying-pan hat and paper-bag boots.
2. Each story in this book contains a moral lesson at the end.
3. Arnold Lobel received the 1981 Caldecott award for this book.

44. (*Fables*)

Caldecott Bingo

The Egg Tree	A Tree Is Nice	Little House	Make Way for Ducklings	The Funny Little Woman
Chanticleer and the Fox	Question **5**	Finders Keepers	Rooster Crows	Question **27**
Biggest Bear	The Little Island	Prayer for a Child	Once A Mouse	Drummer Hoff
Madeline's Rescue	White Snow, Bright Snow	Mei Li	Where the Wild Things Are	Snowy Day
The Song of the Swallows	Many Moons	Question **18**	One Fine Day	May I Bring A Friend?

Newbery Bingo

The Newbery Medal, established in 1921, is given each year to the author of the most distinguished contribution to American children's literature during the preceding year. Newbery books are popular with intermediate and upper grade students.

The best time to play Newbery Bingo is following a unit of instruction in which the teacher has made the books available as a group, has carried out a series of oral reports and discussions on the books, and has promoted them in various ways (see Appendix S).

Purposes and Objectives

1. To encourage students to read Newbery Award books
2. To allow peer influence to work in book promotion

Number of Participants

Any number

Materials Needed

☐ Cardboard or poster board

☐ Individual sets of numbered markers

☐ Envelopes

☐ List of game clues for the teacher's use

Instructions for Making Aid

1. Cut a sufficient number of 10" × 12" game cards from cardboard or poster board.
2. Grid the card into a 5 × 5 pattern with 2" squares (see illustration.)
3. Randomly print the names of twenty-five Newbery Award winning books in the squares. Each card should have the titles arranged in a different way.
4. Cut out game tokens the size of the squares and number them from one to sixty (one for each Newbery book on the list). Make a set for each player.
5. Place the sets of tokens in individual student envelopes

STUDENT DIRECTIONS

1. Take one Newbery Bingo game card and one envelope containing game tokens from the box.

2. Place the game board on your desk and organize the tokens alongside. (If you are missing any of the tokens, tell the teacher.)

3. The teacher will call out the number of a Newbery book and will give the hardest clue first.

4. If you know the book, place the appropriate token over the title on your card.

5. After the hard clues for all titles have been given, the less difficult clues will be called, and finally the author clues.

6. When five titles have been covered in any horizontal or vertical row, the student calls "Bingo."

7. The teacher will match the token numbers with the correct titles to ensure accuracy.

Variations and Teaching Hints

The game can be expanded to include all of the Newbery books, twenty-five at a time. It will be necessary to make new game boards for each twenty-five books.

Storage

The game cards and tokens should be stored away until the teacher is ready to use them with students.

Evaluation

1. Recognition of the titles of books
2. Increased interest in Newbery Award books
3. Wider reading of the award books

CLUES FOR NEWBERY BINGO

1. This is the only history book ever to win the award.
2. This is the first book to receive the Newbery Award.
3. Hendrik Van Loon received the 1922 Newbery Award for this book.

1. (The Story of Mankind)

1. On a voyage to Spidermonkey Island, the hero and his companions are shipwrecked by a violent storm.
2. This man has the ability to talk with animals.
3. Hugh Lofting won the 1923 Newbery Award for this book.

2. (The Voyages of Doctor Dolittle)

1. Philip is finally able to escape a British man-of-war but is not able to convince the captain of his innocence.
2. The ship *The Rose of Devon* is taken over by the Old One and his buccaneers.
3. Charles Boardman Hawes won the 1924 Newbery Award for this book.

3. (The Dark Frigate)

1. There are thirteen stories in this collection of folklore of other countries; right prevails over might.
2. The author of this book traveled from one land to another and shared the stories that were part of each nation's heritage.
3. Charles J. Finger won the 1925 Newbery Award for this book.

4. (Tales from Silver Lands)

1. The author tells humorous stories of Chinese life many years ago.
2. Ah Mu accidently invents a method of printing by smearing his father's carvings with jam.
3. Arthur Bowie Chrisman won the 1926 Newbery Award for this book.

5. (Shen of the Sea)

1. Because he was a one-man horse and because he suffered a great deal of abuse, he became the wildest outlaw on the rodeo circuit.
2. The story of a range pony who had a great deal of horse sense, and a cowboy named Clint who worked with him and trained him to be the best cowhorse on the Rocking *R* Ranch.
3. Will James won the 1927 Newbery Award for this book.

6. (Smoky, the Cowhorse)

1. The message of this book is "Live courage, breathe courage, and give courage."
2. This is the story of a pigeon who encounters many dangers: birds of prey, stormy weather, and bullets.
3. Dhan Gopal Mukerji won the 1928 Newbery Award for this book.

7. (*Gayneck, the Story of a Pigeon*)

1. This story is based on a legend about a thirteenth-century boy whose courage and patriotism still inspire Polish children.
2. A ritual that is still performed in Poland is described in this book.
3. Eric P. Kelly won the 1929 Newbery Award for this book.

8. (*The Trumpeter of Krakow*)

1. Her adventures cover a century of American history.
2. A small doll made from a piece of mountain-ash began her travels around the world in the arms of Phoebe Preble.
3. Rachel Field won the 1930 Newbery Award for this book.

9. (*Hitty, Her First Hundred Years*)

1. The book is composed of a number of legends concerning Buddha and the blessing of the animals.
2. One animal refused to accept the teachings of Buddah and was denied his blessing.
3. Elizabeth Coatsworth won the 1931 Newbery Award for this book.

10. (*The Cat Who Went to Heaven*)

1. This is the story of a young Navaho Indian boy and his experiences as he grows toward maturity.
2. A book of Indian lore and legends.
3. Laura Adams Armer won the 1932 Newbery Award for this book.

11. (*Waterless Mountain*)

1. A young Chinese boy is apprenticed to Tang, the best coppersmith in Chunking.
2. The boy hates Den because Den makes fun of him.
3. Elizabeth Foreman Lewis won the 1933 Newbery Award for this book.

12. (*Young Fu of the Upper Yangtze*)

1. Her first popular writings were letters she wrote home while working in a hospital during the Civil War.

2. This is the story about one of America's most beloved authors.

3. Cornelia Meigs won the 1934 Newbery Award for this book.

13. (*Invincible Louisa*)

1. This is the story of a young boy who grows to manhood with the help of a loving grandfather, a self-sacrificing mother, and a girl who is to become his wife.

2. The boy is to dive for the golden cross on the feast of Saint John the Baptist.

3. Monica Shannon won the 1935 Newbery Award for this book.

14. (*Dobry*)

1. This is a story of a tomboy girl who runs with her brothers.

2. This is a story of a young girl and her family living on the Wisconsin frontier.

3. Carol Brink won the 1936 Newbery Award for this book.

15. (*Caddie Woodlawn*)

1. This is a story about old New York and a ten-year-old girl who spent the summer there.

2. Lucinda's adventures begin when her family goes to Europe and leaves her with her aunts.

3. Ruth Sawyer won the 1937 Newbery Award for this book.

16. (*Roller Skates*)

1. This story traces the generation of tribal leaders from Old Nimrod to his two sons Hun and Magyar.

2. He was the largest, most beautiful animal anyone had ever seen.

3. Kate Seredy won the 1938 Newbery Award for this book.

17. (*The White Stag*)

1. Many of Garnet Linden's adventures stemmed from the natural happenings of a farm summer.

2. In this book, two girls found themselves locked up when they were unnoticed while reading in the library.

3. Elizabeth Enright won the 1939 Newbery Award for this book.

18. (*Thimble Summer*)

1. For many years he trapped, hunted, and explored Kentucky and the land west of the Appalachian Mountains.

2. One of America's most popular folk heroes is portrayed in this book.

3. James H. Daugherty won the 1940 Newbery Award for this book.

19. (Daniel Boone)

1. Alone in his canoe, Mafatu paddles out to sea to conquer his fear of the ocean.
2. Mafatu's name means *Stout Heart*, but the village people call him a coward.
3. Armstrong Sperry received the 1941 Newbery Award for this book.

20. (Call It Courage)

1. This story is about how young Edward saved his family and became a hero during the French and Indian war.
2. On the mantle above the fireplace was a gun "as long as a man is tall."
3. Walter D. Edmonds won the 1942 Newbery Award for this book.

21. (The Matchlock Gun)

1. A young minstrel and his dog share many adventures as they travel through thirteenth-century England.
2. A boy and his dog search over the English countryside for the boy's father.
3. Elizabeth Janet Gray won the 1943 Newbery Award for this book.

22. (Adam of the Road)

1. Apprenticed to a silversmith, a young man exhibits talent and leadership, but little tact.
2. A crucible of molten silver breaks, burning his right hand. He gives up silver work and becomes a messenger for the leaders of the American Revolution.
3. Esther Forbes received the 1944 Newbery Award for this book.

23. (Johhny Tremain)

1. This is a story of Little Georgie and his family.
2. The animals are worried about new folks moving into the big house.
3. Robert Lawson received the 1945 Newbery Award for this book.

24. (Rabbit Hill)

1. All of the conversation in this book is in the dialect of Florida *Crackers*.
2. This story is about the problems the Boyer family have with their neighbors, the Slaters.
3. Lois Lenski received the 1946 Newbery Award for this book.

25. (Strawberry Girl)

1. She has friends among the birds and animals of the woods, but also a few enemies.
2. This is the tale of a doll made from an apple twig.
3. Carolyn Sherwin Bailey received the 1947 Newbery Award for this book.

26. (*Miss Hickory*)

1. Professor Sherman sets out to spend a year in his airborne home.
2. The professor manages to land on Krakatoa and becomes an honored guest.
3. William Pene du Bois received the 1948 Newbery Award for this book.

27. (*The Twenty-One Balloons*)

1. The Earl of Godolphin claims Sham and his mute helper Agba for his own.
2. Sham was born with both the symbols of *swiftness* and *ill-fortune*.
3. Marguerite Henry received the 1949 Newbery Award for this book.

28. (*King of the Wind*)

1. This is the story of a crippled boy who overcomes physical and emotional obstacles to become a knight.
2. No matter how hard life becomes, there is always a way out.
3. Marguerite de Angeli received the 1950 Newbery Award for this book.

29. (*The Door in the Wall*)

1. A royal man from Africa is sold into slavery in America.
2. He learns a trade and buys his own freedom.
3. Elizabeth Yates received the 1951 Newbery Award for this book.

30. (*Amos Fortune, Free Man*)

1. An old yellow hat becomes an important clue in this mystery story.
2. Finally, after months of searching, Bennie finds his stolen dog.
3. Eleanor Estes received the 1952 Newbery Award for this book.

31. (*Ginger Pye*)

1. Cusi, an Indian boy, is about to make his first trip into civilization.
2. Chuto tells Cusi that certain knowledge cannot be explained.
3. Ann Nolan Clark received the 1953 Newbery Award for this book.

32. (*Secret of the Andes*)

1. A young boy prays to be allowed to go with his father into the mountains.

2. This story tells what it is like to be a *middle* child, between a younger and older brother.
3. Joseph Krumgold received the 1954 Newbery Award for this book.

33. (. . . *and now Miguel*)

1. Shora, the setting for this story, is a small fishing village in Holland.
2. Lina and the other schoolchildren set out to bring the storks back to Shora.
3. Meindert DeJong received the 1955 Newbery Award for this book.

34. (*The Wheel on the School*)

1. Nat's seagoing family lived in Salem in the 1780s; he has two dreams—to go to sea and to go to Harvard.
2. While aboard the ships, Nat learns many languages and writes a book on navigation that is still used.
3. Jean Latham received the 1956 Newbery Award for this book.

35. (*Carry on Mr. Bowditch*)

1. The bickering and unhappiness between Joe and Marly gives way to love and consideration for each other.
2. The midnight rescue of a family of foxes, the unexpected visit of a hermit, the gathering of maple syrup are all part of this story.
3. Virginia Sorenson received the 1957 Newbery Award for this book.

36. (*Miracles on Maple Hill*)

1. Sixteen-year-old Jefferson Davis Bussey joins the Kansas Volunteers at the start of the Civil War.
2. Jeff's bravery in battle won him the Medal of Honor; his sensitivity won him the love of Lucy, the beautiful rebel girl.
3. Harold Keith received the 1958 Newbery Award for this book.

37. (*Rifles for Waite*)

1. This is a novel of politics, religion, witchcraft, Puritan ethics, and romance.
2. In this book, Kit is accused of being a witch and is tried because she can swim, and women are not supposed to be able to do that.
3. Elizabeth George Speare received the 1959 Newbery Award for this book.

38. (*The Witch of Blackbird Pond*)

1. This story is about a strange man who lives by himself and speaks a language of his own.

2. In this book, "John ate onions the way Andy ate apples."

3. Joseph Krumgold received the 1960 Newbery Award for this book.

39. (*Onion John*)

1. This novel is a feminine version of Robinson Crusoe.

2. Karana keeps herself alive by building a shelter, making weapons, finding food, and fighting off the wild dogs.

3. Scott O'Dell received the 1961 Newbery Award for this book.

40. (*Island of the Blue Dolphins*)

1. From the day Daniel saw his father killed, he lived for a time that he could help drive the Romans from his country.

2. Daniel runs away and lives on the mountains with Rosh and a group of outlaws that he believes will free the Jews from the Romans.

3. Elizabeth George Speare received the 1962 Newbery Award for this book.

41. (*The Bronze Bow*)

1. This is a science fiction book about a pulsating brain that controls everyone.

2. The children travel into outer space by *tesseract* and meet some unusual characters—Mrs. Whatsit, Mrs. Who, and Mrs. Which.

3. Madeleine L'Engle received the 1963 Newbery Award for this book.

42. (*A Wrinkle in Time*)

1. This is a story of a fourteen-year-old boy growing up in the New York City area—Gramercy Park, Coney Island, the Fulton Fish Market, and the Bronx Zoo.

2. Dave Mitchell grows to understand his parents and to get along with them a little better.

3. Emily Neville received the 1964 Newbery Award for this book.

43. (*It's Like This, Cat*)

1. Manolo takes the advice of an old friend of his father who tells him to be himself and do what is right for him.

2. Manolo Olivar decides, against the wishes of his village, not to follow in his father's footsteps.

3. Maia Wojciechowska received the 1965 Newbery Award for this book.

44. (*Shadow of a Bull*)

1. The trusted servant of a court painter of seventeenth-century Spain learns to paint, which is forbidden because he is a slave.

2. His master gives him freedom so that he will not be imprisoned, and the slave becomes a great artist.

3. Elizabeth Borton de Trevino received the 1966 Newbery Award for this book.

45. (I, Juan de Pareja)

1. At age seven, Julie has to face the death of her mother.

2. Julie falls out of love with Brett after she discovers that he is interested only in her ability to help him with his schoolwork.

3. Irene Hunt received the 1967 Newbery Award for this book.

46. (Up a Road Slowly)

1. In this book, two children run away from home and spend a whole week in the Museum of Modern Art in New York City.

2. Claudia and James learn, by searching for clues, that the statue called "Angel" was designed by Michelangelo.

3. E. L. Konigsburg received the 1968 Newbery Award for this book.

47. (From the Mixed-Up Files of Mrs. Basil E. Frankweiler)

1. This story is based on a Welch legend—the final struggle between good and evil.

2. Taran and Prince Gwydion raise an army to march against Arawan in a struggle that is the most crucial of their lives.

3. Lloyd Alexander received the 1969 Newbery Award for this book.

48. (The High King)

1. This is a tragic story of a southern family struggling against poverty and prejudice.

2. A boy searches to find his missing father but grows to manhood without him

3. William H. Armstrong received the 1970 Newbery Award for this book.

49. (Sounder)

1. One night Charlie disappears and Sara's small problems are left behind as she searches in the dense woods for her brother.

2. This story is about a teenage girl, Sara, and her love for a retarded brother.

3. Betsy Byars received the 1971 Newbery Award for this book.

50. (The Summer of the Swans)

1. In this novel, laboratory rats are given hormones and develop into geniuses who outwit the scientists.

2. The rats learn to read, find out how to open their cages, and escape the lab; they establish a model community in Mr. Fitzgibbon's garden.

3. Robert C. O'Brien received the 1972 Newbery Award for this book.

51. (*Mrs. Frisby and the Rats of NIMH*)

1. When Miyax runs away and tries to reach Amy, her San Francisco pen pal, she becomes lost in the Tundra.

2. Alone, except for a pack of Arctic wolves, Miyax rethinks her Eskimo past.

3. Jean Craighead George received the 1973 Newbery Award for this book.

52. (*Julie of the Wolves*)

1. Jessie Bollier is kidnapped from New Orleans and carried off to a slave ship because he can play the fife and can help to exercise the slaves.

2. *The Moonlight* is shipwrecked off the coast of Mississippi, and the only survivors are Jessie and Ras, a black slave.

3. Paula Fox received the 1974 Newbery Award for this book.

52. (*The Slave Dancer*)

1. Atop a gleaming forty-foot pole, a young boy watches the waste from a strip mine endanger his home.

2. Two strangers make their way toward Sarah's Mountain, the dude and Lurhetta. Each plays a role in the boy's dreams and destiny.

3. Virginia Hamilton received the 1975 Newbery Award for this book.

54. (*M. C. Higgins, the Great*)

1. There is an old legend in North Wales that within a certain hill, a harp of gold will be found by a boy who is followed by a white dog who can see in the wind.

2. After an unusual illness, Will Scranton meets a strange boy named Bran and a white dog, Cafall.

3. Susan Cooper received the 1976 Newbery Award for this book.

55. (*The Grey King*)

1. The Logans keep their land and maintain their independence despite severe hardships.

2. The Logans were a proud, black family living in Mississippi during the Depression.

3. Mildred D. Taylor received the 1977 Newbery Award for this book.

56. (*Roll of Thunder, Hear My Cry*)

1. Jess Aarons, the fastest runner at Lake Creek elementary School, is defeated in a race by a girl.

2. Jess and Leslie create a secret kingdom in the woods until an unexpected tragedy strikes.

3. Katherine Paterson received the 1978 Newbery Award for this book.

57. (*Bridge to Terabithia*)

Newbery Bingo

Johnny Tremain	Sounder	Story of Mankind	Question 17	Dobry
Question 23	Adam of the Road	Daniel Boone	Invincible Louisa	The Cat Who Went to Heaven
Caddie Woodlawn	Gay-Neck	Shen of the Sea	Question 6	Tales From Silver Lands
Dark Frigate	Call It Courage	White Stag	Question 42	Roller Skates
Waterless Mountain	The Voyages of Dr. Doolittle	High King	Question 30	Rabbit Hill

1. Sixteen people are invited to the reading of a very strange will in this mystery story.
2. Any of the characters can become millionaires, depending on how they play a dangerous game.
3. Ellen Raskin received the 1979 Newbery Award for this book.

58. (*The Westing Game*)

1. "I, Catherine Cabot Hall, aged 13 years, 7 months, 8 days, of Meredith in the state of New Hampshire, do begin this book."
2. This book is a young New England girl's journal.
3. Joan W. Blos received the 1980 Newbery Award for this book.

59. (*A Gathering of Days*)

1. This is a novel by the author of *Bridge to Terabithia*.
2. This story is about Louise who dislikes her selfish twin sister.
3. Katherine Paterson received the 1981 Newbery Award for this book.

60. (*Jacob Have I Loved*)

APPENDICES

DOLCH BASIC
SIGHT WORD LIST

The following 220 words were found by Edward Dolch to be those most frequently encountered by primary children in their reading material. Used by permission.

BREAKDOWN OF LIST BY LEVELS

PREPRIMER	PRIMER	FIRST GRADE	SECOND GRADE	THIRD GRADE
1. a	1. all	1. after	1. always	1. about
2. and	2. am	2. again	2. around	2. better
3. away	3. are	3. an	3. because	3. bring
4. big	4. at	4. any	4. been	4. carry
5. blue	5. ate	5. as	5. before	5. clean
6. came	6. be	6. ask	6. best	6. cut
7. can	7. black	7. by	7. both	7. done
8. come	8. brown	8. could	8. buy	8. draw
9. find	9. but	9. every	9. call	9. drink
10. for	10. came	10. fly	10. cold	10. eight
11. funny	11. did	11. from	11. does	11. fall
12. go	12. go	12. give	12. don't	12. far
13. help	13. eat	13. going	13. fast	13. full

PREPRIMER	PRIMER	FIRST GRADE	SECOND GRADE	THIRD GRADE
14. here	14. four	14. had	14. first	14. got
15. I	15. get	15. has	15. five	15. grow
16. in	16. good	16. her	16. found	16. hold
17. is	17. have	17. him	17. gave	17. hot
18. it	18. he	18. his	18. goes	18. hurt
19. jump	19. into	19. how	19. green	19. if
20. little	20. like	20. just	20. its	20. keep
21. look	21. must	21. know	21. made	21. kind
22. make	22. new	22. let	22. many	22. laugh
23. me	23. no	23. live	23. off	23. light
24. my	24. now	24. may	24. or	24. long
25. not	25. on	25. of	25. pull	25. much
26. one	26. our	26. old	26. read	26. myself
27. play	27. out	27. once	27. right	27. never
28. red	28. please	28. open	28. sing	28. only
29. run	29. pretty	29. over	29. sit	29. own
30. said	30. run	30. put	30. sleep	30. pick
31. see	31. ride	31. round	31. tell	31. seven
32. the	32. saw	32. some	32. their	32. shall
33. three	33. say	33. stop	33. these	33. show
34. to	34. she	34. take	34. those	34. six
35. two	35. so	35. thank	35. up	35. small
36. up	36. soon	36. them	36. upon	36. start
37. we	37. that	37. then	37. use	37. ten
38. where	38. there	38. think	38. very	38. today
39. yellow	39. they	39. walk	39. wash	39. together
40. you	40. this	40. were	40. which	40. try
	41. too	41. when	41. why	41. warm
	42. under		42. wish	
	43. want		43. work	
	44. was		44. would	
	45. well		45. write	
	46. went		46. your	

PREPRIMER	PRIMER	FIRST GRADE	SECOND GRADE	THIRD GRADE
	47. what			
	48. white			
	49. who			
	50. will			
	51. with			
	52. yes			

APPENDIX B
FREQUENTLY USED NOUNS

From primary readers, standardized tests for primary grades, trade books for young children, and school newspapers, R. Van Allen isolated the following list of 230 nouns. Used by permission.

air	body	clock	ear	food	horse
airplane	book	clothes	earth	forest	house
animal	box	clown	egg	four	
answer	boys	coat	elephant	fox	ice cream
apartment	bread	cookies	end	frame	island
apple	breakfast	corner	example	friend	
astronaut	brother	country	eyes	frog	jacket
author	bus	cow		front	Jack-o'-lantern
		cup	fall		jelly
baby	cake		family	game	
ball	candy	daddy	father	garden	king
balloon	cap	day	feet	girl	kite
basement	car	dime	field	grass	
bear	cat	dog	fire	ground	lamp
bed	chair	dollar	first	guitar	land
bee	chicken	door	fish		leaf
bell	children	dress	five	hand	leg
bird	church	drum	flag	head	letter
block	circle	duck	floor	hill	life
boat	city		flower	home	light

line	one	queen	shoe	sun	wall
lion	orange		show	swing	water
lunch		rabbit	side		way
	page	rain	sister	table	whistle
man	palace	raincoat	sky	tail	white
men	paper	refrigerator	sleep	teacher	wind
miles	part	river	snow	telephone	window
milk	pencil	road	sock	television	winter
money	penny	rock	something	thing	witch
monkey	people	rocket	song	three	woman
moon	pet	roof	sound	time	word
morning	picture	room	spring	today	world
mother	pilot	rope	square	tooth	
mouth	place	rose	stairs	top	x-ray
	play		stamp	town	store
name	poem	sailboat	star	tree	yard
nest	point	school	stop sign	truck	year
next	policeman	sea	store	turkey	
nickel	pony	second	story	two	zipper
night	princess	sentence	stove		zoo
nose	purse	sheet	street	umbrella	
nurse		ship	summer		
	quarter	shirt		valentine	

APPENDIX C

WORD FAMILIES
FOR SUBSTITUTION
OF INITIAL
CONSONANT SOUNDS

back	pack	stack	brag
black	rack	tack	drag
crack	sack	track	flag
Jack	shack		gag
lack	slack	bag	lag

nag	frail	brain	trap
rag	hail	drain	
sag	jail	gain	bat
snag	mail	grain	brat
tag	nail	lain	cat
wag	pail	main	fat
	rail	pain	flat
best	sail	plain	hat
blest	snail	rain	mat
crest	tail	train	pat
lest	trail	vain	rat
nest			sat
pest	bet	bunk	scat
rest	fret	drunk	
test	get	dunk	bell
vest	jet	flunk	fell
zest	let	hunk	sell
	met	junk	shell
bold	net	skunk	smell
cold	pet	spunk	spell
fold	set	sunk	swell
gold	wet	trunk	tell
hold			well
mold	crop	bed	yell
scold	drop	bled	
sold	flop	fed	buck
told	hop	fled	duck
	mop	led	luck
bake	pop	Ned	pluck
brake	shop	red	struck
cake	stop	sled	stuck
fake	top	Ted	suck
flake			truck
Jake	clay	cap	tuck
lake	day	clap	
make	gay	flap	bug
rake	hay	gap	chug
sake	lay	lap	drug
shake	may	map	dug
snake	pay	nap	hug
take	play	rap	jug
wake	ray	slap	mug
	say	snap	plug
bail	stray	strap	rug
fail	tray	tap	slug
	way		smug

snug	sank	not	kick
tug	spank	pot	lick
	tank	plot	nick
bump	thank	shot	pick
chump		slot	sick
dump	bran	spot	slick
hump	can	trot	stick
jump	clan		thick
lump	Dan	blame	trick
plump	fan	came⁻	
pump	man	dame	Bill
slump	pan	fame	drill
stump	plan	flame	fill
thump	ran	frame	hill
	tan	game	kill
bit	van	lame	mill
fit		name	pill
flit	brim	same	skill
grit	dim	tame	spill
hit	grim		still
pit	him	clear	will
sit	Jim	dear	
slit	rim	fear	bad
split	slim	hear	dad
wit	swim	near	fad
	Tim	rear	glad
band	trim	smear	had
brand		spear	lad
gland	beat	tear	mad
grand	cheat	year	pad
hand	heat		sad
land	meat	bend	
sand	neat	blend	ball
stand	seat	lend	call
	treat	mend	fall
bank	wheat	send	hall
blank		spend	mall
crank	blot	tend	small
flank	cot		stall
frank	dot	brick	tall
plank	got	chick	wall
prank	hot	click	
rank	lot	Dick	bun

run	fun
spun	gun
stun	nun
sun	pun

APPENDIX D
PREFIXES

A *prefix* is a sound attached to the beginning of a word and serves to produce a derivative word.

PREFIX	DEFINITION	EXAMPLE
ab-	from, away	absent
ad-	to, toward	adore
anti-	against, opposite	antifreeze
auto-	self	autobiography
bi-	two	bicycle
bio-	life	biology
cent-	hundred	century
circum-	around	circumstance
co-, con-	with, together	cooperate
contra-	against	contrary
counter-	against	counterattack
de-	from, down	depart
dis-	apart, away	distant
en-	to give	enjoy
ex-	out, of, from, formerly	express
fore-	before	forewarn

PREFIX	DEFINITION	EXAMPLE
hemi-	half	hemisphere
in-	negative, in	indirect
inter-	between, among	international
intra-	within	intrastate
mal-	wrong or bad	malpractice
micro-	very small	microscope
mid-	halfway	midpoint
mis-	negative	misfortune
mono-	one, single	monograph
per-	through	perforate
post-	after	postscript
pre-	before	preview
pro-	for, before	program
quad-	four	quadrangle
re-	again, against	repay
sub-	under, beneath	submarine
super-	above, in excess	superhighway
tele-	far	television
trans-	across, through	transportation
tri-	three	trimotor
un-	negative	unnatural
uni-	one	unify

APPENDIX E
SUFFIXES

A *suffix* is a sound attached to the end of a word and serves to produce a derivative word.

SUFFIX	DEFINITION	EXAMPLE
-al	pertaining to	personal
-ance	action, quality, state	inheritance
-ant	one who	descendant
-ate	act, furnish	evaporate
-able	capable of, fitness	lovable
-cy	action, practice, state, or quality	truancy
-er, or	one who, process of	New Yorker
-ful	full of, characterized by	graceful
-ial	quality of	jovial
-ic	belonging	volcanic
-ion	condition, state, or process of	fusion
-ish	belonging to	childish
-ist	person who does, is skilled, professes a doctrine	druggist
-ity	state, quality, degree	sanity
-ive	condition, state, or quality of	selective
-ly	in the manner of	lonely
-ous	full of, having the quality of	dangerous
-sion	condition, state, or quality of	suspension
-tion	condition, state, or quality of	creation
-tude	condition, state, or quality of	certitude

APPENDIX F
COMPOUND WORDS

A *compound word* is a word consisting of components that are words. Each part of a compound word retains its original meaning.

afternoon	battlefield	bookkeeper
aircraft	battleship	bookmark
airline	bedroll	bookstore
airplane	bedroom	bookworm
airport	bedside	brainstorm
anthill	bedspread	breakdown
anybody	bedtime	bridegroom
anyhow	beeswax	broadcast
anyone	bellhop	broomstick
anyplace	beside	bulldog
anything	birdhouse	bullfrog
anytime	birthday	buttercup
anyway	birthplace	butterfly
anywhere	birthstone	buttermilk
armchair	blackberry	butterscotch
automobile	blackbird	
	blacksmith	campsite
backdoor	blastoff	candlestick
bandstand	blowout	cannot
bareback	bluebell	cardboard
barefoot	blueberry	catfish
barnyard	bluebird	chairman
baseball	blueprint	championship
basketball	boatman	chessboard
bathroom	bodyguard	classmate
bathtile	bookcase	classroom
bathtub		clockwise

clubhouse
coastline
cookbook
cornfield
countdown
counterclockwise
countryside
courthouse
cowboy
cowgirl
crosswalk
cupcake

daredevil
daytime
dishcloth
dishpan
dishtowel
dishwater
dogwater
doghouse
doorbell
doorman
doorstep
doorway
doughnut
downpour
downstairs
dragonfly
drawbridge
dressmaker
driveway
drugstore
dugout

evergreen
everybody
everyone
everything
eyeball
eyebrow
eyelid
eyesight

farmhouse
firearms
fireman
fireplace
fireside
firewood
filmstrip
fingernail
fingertip
fisherman
fishhook
flagpole
floodlight
football
footman
footstep
footstool
friendship
fullback

gingerbread
goldenrod
gooseberry
grandfather
grandmother
grandstand
grapefruit

grapevine
grasshopper
graveyard
greenhouse

hairbrush
hallway
handbag
handbook
handmade
handwriting
hatbox
headmaster
henhouse
herself
highpower
highway
himself
hitchhike
horseback
horseshoe
houseboat
housewife
however
hummingbird

inside
into

jackknife
jellyfish

keyhole
kingfish

landlord

lifeboat

lifejacket

lifetime

lighthouse

lonesome

loophole

lunchroom

mailman

manpower

marksman

maybe

meanwhile

milkman

milkweed

moonlight

motorboat

motorcycle

mountainside

necktie

neighborhood

network

newsprint

nightgown

nightmare

nighttime

northwest

notebook

nowhere

oatmeal

oceanfront

oceanliner

oilcloth

otherwise

outboard

outside

overboard

overgrown

pancake

paperback

peacetime

peppermint

pigsty

pigtail

pineapple

pitchfork

playground

playhouse

playmate

playpen

pocketbook

popcorn

porthole

proofread

railroad

rainbow

raincoat

rainstorm

redcap

riverbank

rowboat

sailboat

salesman

sandbox

sandman

sandpaper

schoolbook

schoolhouse

schoolyard

scoreboard

scorekeeper

seaplane

seaport

seashell

seashore

sharpshooter

shipwreck

shoehorn

shoelace

shoemaker

shoreline

shortbread

shortstop

sidewalk

silkworm

slowpoke

snapdragon

snowfight

snowflake

snowman

snowplow

snowshoe

snowstorm

somehow

someone

something

sometimes

somewhere

swordfish

spaceman

spellbound

starfish

steamboat

steamroller

steamshovel

stoplight

storybook

strawberry

streetcar

sunflower

sunshine

supermarket

swordfish

tablecloth

taxpayer

teammate

textbook

Thanksgiving

tiptoe

today

tonight

toothache

toothbrush

toothpaste

typewriter

underground

undersize

understood

upset

upstairs

uptown

watchman

waterproof

whenever

whichever

windmill

windshield

without

workbook

workshop

worldwide

yardstick

zookeeper

APPENDIX G

CONTRACTIONS

A *contraction* is the shortening of a word by omitting a sound or letter.

aren't

can't

couldn't

didn't

doesn't

don't

hasn't

haven't

he'd

he'll

he's

how'd

how'll

how's

I'd

I'll

I'm

I've

isn't

it'll

it's

let's

she'd

she'll

she's	wasn't	where's
shouldn't	we'd	who'll
	we'll	who'd
that'd, that'll	we're	won't
that's	weren't	wouldn't
there'd	we've	
there'll	what'd	you'll
there's	what'll	you're
they'd	what's	you've
they'll	where'd	
they're	where'll	

APPENDIX H
COMMON ABBREVIATIONS

An *abbreviation* is a shortened form of a word or phrase.

A.B.C. — American Broadcasting Company

A.D. — In the year of the Lord

A.M. — Ante Meridiem

Apr. — April

Assn. — Association

Aug. — August

Ave. — Avenue

B.A. — Bachelor of Arts

B.C. — Before Christ

Blvd. — Boulevard

B.S. — Bachelor of Science

C.B.S. — Columbia Broadcasting System

Co. — Company

C.O.D. — Cash on Delivery

Corp. — Corporation

Dec. — December

Dr. — Doctor

Dr. — Drive

E. — East

Elem. — Elementary

Feb. — February

Fri. — Friday

Ft. — Foot

Gal. — Gallon

Gen. — General

Gov. — Governor

Hr. — Hour

H.S. — High School

I.D. — Identification

In. — Inch

Inc. — Incorporated

Jan. — January

Jr. — Junior

Jr.H. — Junior High

Lb. — Pound

Ltd. — Limited

M.A. — Master of Arts

Mar. — March

Min. — Minute

Mon. — Monday

Mr. — Mister

Mrs. — Mistress

M.S. — Master of Science

N. — North

N.B.A. — National Basketball Association

N.B.C. — National Broadcasting Company

N.F.L. — National Football League

Nov. — November

Oct. — October

Oz. — Ounce

Ph.D. — Doctor of Philosophy

P.M. — Post Meridian

P.O. — Post Office

Pres. — President

Prof. — Professor

Pt. — Pint

P.T.A. — Parent-Teacher Association

Q.B. — Quarterback

Qt. — Quart

Rd. — Road

Rev. — Reverend

R.F.D. — Rural Free Delivery

R.N. — Registered Nurse

R.R. — Railroad

S. — South

Sat. — Saturday

Sec. — Second

Sec. — Secondary

Sec. — Secretary

Sen. — Senator

Sept. — September

Sgt. — Sergeant

Sr. — Senior

St. — Street

Sun. — Sunday

T.D. — Touchdown

Thur. — Thursday

Tue. — Tuesday

T.V. — Television

U.P.S. — United Parcel Service

U.S.A. — United States of America   Wed. — Wednesday

V.P. — Vice-President   Yd. — Yard

W. — West

ABBREVIATIONS
OF STATE NAMES
AND TERRITORIES

AL — Alabama

AK — Alaska

AZ — Arizona

AR — Arkansas

CA — California

CO — Colorado

CT — Connecticut

DE — Delaware

DC — District of Columbia

FL — Florida

GA — Georgia

GU — Guam

HI — Hawaii

ID — Idaho

IL — Illinois

IN — Indiana

IA — Iowa

KS — Kansas

KY — Kentucky

LA — Louisiana

ME — Maine

MD — Maryland

MA — Massachusetts

MI — Michigan

MN — Minnesota

MS — Mississippi

MO — Missouri

MT — Montana

NB — Nebraska

NV — Nevada

NH — New Hampshire

NJ — New Jersey

NM — New Mexico

NY — New York

NC — North Carolina

ND — North Dakota

OH — Ohio

OK — Oklahoma

OR — Oregon

PA — Pennsylvania

PR — Puerto Rico

RI — Rhode Island

SC — South Carolina
SD — South Dakota
TN — Tennessee
TX — Texas
UT — Utah
VT — Vermont

VA — Virginia
VI — Virgin Islands
WA — Washington
WV — West Virginia
WI — Wisconsin
WY — Wyoming

APPENDIX I
ANTONYMS

An *antonym* is a word of opposite meaning.

alive, dead
all, none
always, never
arm, leg
aunt, uncle
awake, asleep

back, front
before, after
begin, end
best, worst
big, little
black, white
bold, cowardly
borrow, loan
brother, sister
buy, sell

came, went
children, adults

close, open
cool, warm

dangerous, safe
dark, light
day, night
deep, shallow
dim, bright
dirty, clean

east, west
easy, hard
empty, full
engine, caboose
enter, exit
everything, nothing

fast, slow
fat, thin
few, many

fingers, toes
first, last
for, against

gigantic, wee
girl, boy
good, bad

happy, sad
hard, soft
head, foot
here, there
high, low
honesty, deceit
hot, cold
husband, wife

ill, healthy
in, out

jam, release
just, unfair
justify, blame

keen, dull
king, queen

late, early
laugh, cry
lead, follow
left, right
long, short
lost, found

male, female
morning, evening

narrow, wide
need, have
near, far
niece, nephew
north, south

old, new

plain, fancy
pointed, rounded
pretty, ugly
prince, princess

proud, humble
push, pull

quiet, noisy

raw, cooked
real, fake
rich, poor
rough, smooth
round, square
run, walk

same, different
sharp, dull
short, tall
shout, whisper
sick, well
simple, complex
small, large
smile, frown
son, daughter
stand, sit
stay, leave
straight, crooked
strange, familiar
stretch, shrink
summer, winter
sun, moon

sunny, rainy
sunrise, sunset
sweet, sour

take, give
tell, listen
throw, catch
together, apart
top, bottom
true, false

under, over
up, down

vacant, full
vain, modest
victory, defeat

weak, strong
wet, dry
will, won't
woman, man
won, lost
work, play

young, old
you, me
yes, no

APPENDIX J
HOMOPHONES

A *homophone* is one of two or more words pronounced alike but different in meaning.

acts, ax, axe

air, heir

aisle, isle, I'll

aloud, allowed

Ann, an

ant, aunt

ate, eight

aye, eye, I

ball, bawl

bare, bear

beach, beech

beat, beet

bee, be

been, bin

berry, bury

berth, birth

billed, build

blew, blue

board, bored

border, boarder

bore, boar

bow, bough

boy, buoy

bred, bread

but, butt

buy, by, bye

capital, capitol

cell, sell

cellar, seller

cent, sent, scent

chance, chants

chews, choose

choo, chew

claws, clause

climb, clime

close, clothes

colonel, kernel

course, coarse

creak, creek

crewel, cruel

crews, cruise, cruse

days, daze

dear, deer

dents, dense

die, dye

do, dew, due

doe, dough

done, dun

earn, urn

ewe, yew, you

fair, fare

fairy, ferry

feet, feat

find, fined

fir, fur

flea, flee

flew, flue

flour, flower

for, four

forth, fourth

gait, gate

gamble, gambol

gilt, guilt

gourd, gored

grate, great

grater, greater

Greece, grease

groan, grown

guessed, guest

hail, hale

hair, hare

hall, haul

heal, heel

hear, here

heard, herd

hew, hue

higher, hire

him, hymn

hoarse, horse

hole, whole

holy, wholly

hour, our

idol, idle, idyl

inn, in

jam, jamb

key, quay

knap, nap

knead, need, kneed

knew, gnu, new

knight, night

knot, not

know, no

knows, nose

lack, lac

lacks, lax

lain, lane

lead, led

leak, leek

lean, lien

lends, lens

lesson, lessen

load, lode

made, maid

mail, male

main, mane

mare, mayor

marry, merry

marshal, martial

meddle, medal

might, mite

missed, mist

more, mower

morn, mourn

mule, mewl

mustard, mustered

nay, neigh

none, nun

oar, ore

oh, O, owe

one, won

ought, aught

owed, ode

paced, paste

packed, pact

pail, pale

pain, pane

pair, pare, pear

past, passed

patience, patients

paws, pause

peace, piece

peak, peek

peal, peel

pearl, purl

pedal, peddle

plain, plane

pleas, please

pole, poll

pore, pour

praise, prays

presence, presents

pries, prize

principal, principle

prints, prince

quarts, quartz

quire, choir

rain, reign, rein

raise, rays, raze

raiser, razor

rap, wrap

read, reed

real, reel

reck, wreck

red, read

right, rite

ring, wring

road, rode, rowed

Rome, roam

rough, ruff

rye, wry

sail, sale

sane, seine

saver, savor

scene, seen

sea, see

seal, ceil

seam, seem

seas, sees, seize

shear, sheer

shoe, shoo

sight, site, cite

so, sow, sew

soar, sore

some, sum
son, sun
sown, sewn
stair, stare
stake, steak
stationary, stationery
steel, steal
straight, strait
symbol, cymbal

tale, tail
tare, tear
tea, tee
team, teem
tear, tier
teas, tease

tense, tents
the, thee
their, there
threw, through
thrown, throne
thyme, time
tic, tick
tide, tied
toad, toed, towed
toe, tow
told, tolled
too, to, two
tun, ton

use, yews, ewes

vale, veil

vane, vein, vain
vice, vise

wade, weighed
waist, waste
wait, weight
waive, wave
want, wont
ware, wear
way, weigh
we, wee
weak, week
wood, would
wretch, retch
write, wright

yolk, yoke

APPENDIX K
RHYMING WORDS

-ab
cab
gab
nab
slab

-ack
back
black
crack
jack
pack

shack
smack

-act
act
fact
pact

-ad
add
bad
dad

fad
gad
glad
had
lad
mad
sad

-ade
fade
grade
made

shade
spade
trade
wade

-ag
bag
brag
drag
flag
gag
rag
sag

snag

tag

wag

-age

age

cage

page

rage

wage

-ail

fail

hail

jail

mail

nail

rail

sail

snail

tail

-aint

faint

paint

saint

-ake

bake

cake

fake

lake

make

snake

take

wake

-alk

chalk

talk

walk

-all

ball

call

fall

hall

small

tall

wall

-am

dam

ham

jam

ram

-ame

came

dame

fame

flame

lame

name

tame

same

shame

became

-amp

camp

lamp

ramp

stamp

tramp

-an

ban

can

fan

man

pan

-an

plan

ran

tan

van

began

-and

band

brand

gland

grand

hand

land

rand

sand

stand

-ane

cane

lane

airplane

-ang

bang

clang

fang

gang

hang

rang

sang

-ank

bank

drank

plank

prank

rank

sank

spank

tank

thank

yank

-ant

chant

grant

pant

plant

slant

-ap

cap

chap

clap

gap

lap

map

nap

sap

slap

snap

strap

tap

trap

-ape

cape

drape

grape

tape

-ar

bar

car

far

jar

star

tar

guitar

-ark

ark

bark

dark

hark

lark
mark
park
shark
remark

-art

cart
chart
dart
part
smart
start

-ash

bash
cash
dash
crash
flash
hash
lash
mash
rash
slash
smash
trash

-ast

blast
cast
fast
last
mast
past

-aw

claw
draw
flaw
jaw
law
paw

raw
saw
straw

-awn

dawn
fawn
lawn
yawn

-ax

tax
wax
relax

-ay

bay
clay
day
hay
lay
may
pay
play
pray
ray
say
stray
way
away

-aze

blaze
daze
graze
gaze
haze
maze

-each

beach
each
peach

reach
teach

-eam

beam
cream
dream
gleam
scream
stream
team

-ean

bean
clean
lean

-eat

beat
cheat
eat
heat
meat
neat
seat
treat

-eck

check
deck
neck
speck
wreck

-ed

bed
bled
bread
dead
fed
led
red
shed

sled
wed

-ee

be
bee
flee
free
he
me
see
three
tree
we

-eed

bleed
breed
deed
feed
need
seed
weed

-eek

cheek
creek
meek
seek
week

-eep

cheep
creep
deep
peep
seep
sheep
sleep
steep
weep

-ell

bell
cell
dell
dwell
fell
sell
smell
spell
swell
tell
well
yell

-en

den
hen
men
pen
ten
then
when

-end

bend
blend
end
friend
lend
mend
send
spend
tend
trend
attend
defend
depend

-ent

bent
cent
rent
sent

spent
tent
vent
went
cement
content
event
invent

-ep

pep
step

-ept

kept
slept
wept

-ess

chess
dress
less
mess
press
stress

-est

best
chest
crest
guest
nest
pest
rest
test
west

-et

bet
get
jet
let
met

net
pet
set
wet

-ib

bib
crib
fib
rib

-ice

dice
ice
lice
mice
nice
price
rice
slice
spice
twice

-ick

brick
chick
click
kick
lick
nick
pick
quick
sick
stick
thick
tick
wick

-id

bid
did
hid
kid

lid
skid
slid

-ide

bride
hide
ride
side
slide
tide
wide

-ief

brief
chief
grief
thief
belief
relief

-ike

hike
like
spike
strike
alike
dislike

-ill

bill
chill
dill
fill
hill
ill
kill
mill
pill
skill
spill
still
will

-im

brim
dim
him
rim
skim
slim
swim
trim

-ime

crime
dime
lime
slime
time

-in

bin
chin
fin
grin
kin
pin
shin
sin
skin
spin
thin
tin
twin
win

-ind

bind
blind
find
hind
kind
mind
rind
wind

behind
remind

-ine

dine
fine
line
mine
nine
pine
shine
vine
wine

-ing

bring
ding
fling
king
ping
ring
sing
sling
spring
sting
string
swing
thing
wing

-ink

blink
brink
clink
drink
ink
link
pink
sink
stink
think
wink

-int

hint
lint
mint
print
tint

-ip

chip
clip
dip
drip
flip
hip
lip
nip
rip
ship
sip
skip
slip
strip
tip
trip
whip

-ipe

gripe
pipe
ripe
stripe
wipe

-ire

fire
hire
tire
wire

-it

bit
fit
hit

kit
knit
lit
pit
quit
sit
spit
split

-ive

dive
drive
five
hive
live
strive

-ix

fix
mix
six

-ob

cob
job
mob
rob
snob
sob

-ock

block
clock
dock
lock
rock
shock
sock
stock

-od

cod
nod

plod
pod

-og

dog
fog
frog
hog
jog
log

-oil

boil
coil
foil
soil
toil

-oke

coke
joke
poke
smoke
spoke

-old

bold
cold
fold
gold
hold
mold
old
scold
sold
told

-one

bone
cone
lone
stone

zone
alone

-ong

long
song
belong

-ook

book
cook
hook
look
shook
took

-ool

cool
drool
fool
pool
school
spool
stool
tool

-oon

moon
noon
balloon
cartoon
cocoon
racoon

-oop

coop
loop
scoop
stoop
troop

-oot

boot
hoot

root
shoot
toot

-op

cop
hop
mop
shop
slop
stop
top

-orn

born
corn
horn
morn
thorn

-oss

boss
cross
loss
moss
toss

-ot

blot
clot
cot
dot
got
hot
lot
not
plot
pot
rot
shot
slot
spot
tot

-ound

bound
found
ground
hound
mound
pound
round
sound

-our

flour
hour
our
sour

-ouse

blouse
house
mouse

-ow

bow
cow
how
now
brow
plow

-ow

blow
flow
glow
grow
know
low
mow
row
show
slow
snow
below

-own

brown
clown
drown
down
frown
gown
town

-oy

boy
joy
toy
enjoy

-ub

club
cub
hub
scrub
stub
tub

-uck

duck
buck
chuck
luck
struck
stuck
tuck

-uff

bluff
cuff

fluff
gruff
huff
muff
puff
stuff

-ug

bug
drug
dug
hug
jug
mug
plug
rug
snug
thug
tug

-ull

dull
gull
hull
lull
skull

-um

chum
drum
gum
hum
rum

scum
slum
sum

-ump

bump
dump
hump
jump
lump
plump
pump
slump
stump
thump

-un

bun
fun
gun
run
spun
sun

-unch

bunch
crunch
hunch
lunch
munch
punch

-ung

hung
lung

sprung
strung
stung
sung

-unk

bunk
drunk
hunk
junk
skunk
sunk
trunk

-y

buy
by
cry
dry
fly
fry
guy
my
sky
sly
spry
spy
sty
try
why
July
rely

APPENDIX L
POPULAR ACRONYMS

An *acronym* is a word formed from the initial letters of a name, or by combining initial letters or parts of a series of words.

ACE — Army Corps of Engineers

ALCOA — Aluminum Company of America

ARAMCO — Arabian-American Oil Company

ASAP — As Soon As Possible

AWOL — Absent Without Official Leave

BMOC — Big Man on Campus

BOSOX — Boston Red Sox (Baseball team)

CARE — Cooperative for American Relief Everywhere

CHIPS — California Highway Patrol

COP — Constable on Patrol

CORE — Congress of Racial Equality

GIGO — Garbage In, Garbage Out (Computer)

HIFI — High Fidelity

HUD — Department of Housing and Urban Development

JEEP — General Purpose Vehicle

LASER — Light Amplification by Stimulated Emission of Radiation

LULAC — League of United Latin American Citizens

MASH — Mobile Army Surgical Hospital

MOTEL — Motor Hotel

MOPED — Motorized Pedals

NABISCO — National Biscuit Company

NASA — National Aeronautics and Space Administration

NATO — North Atlantic Treaty Organization

NOW — National Organization for Women

OPEC — Organization of Petroleum Exporting Countries

PUSH — People United to Save Humanity

RADAR — Radio Detection and Ranging

RIF — Reading Is Fundamental

SALT — Strategic Arms Limitation Talks

SCIFI — Science Fiction

SCUBA — Self Contained Underwater Breathing Apparatus

SNAFU — Situation Normal All Fouled Up

SONAR — Sound, Navigation, and Ranging

SWAK — Sealed with a Kiss

SWAT — Special Weapons and Tactics

UFO — Unidentified Flying Object

UNESCO — United Nations Educational, Scientific, Cultural Organization

UNIVAC — Universal Automatic Computer

ZIP — Zone Improvement Plan (Postal System)

APPENDIX M
WILSON'S ESSENTIAL VOCABULARY

Recognition of the following words and phrases is considered essential to physical safety and social acceptability. Reprinted with permission of Corlett Wilson and the International Reading Association.

ADULTS ONLY

ALL CARS (TRUCKS) STOP

ANTIDOTE

ASK ATTENDANT FOR KEY

BEWARE

BEWARE OF CROSS WINDS

BEWARE OF THE DOG

BRIDGE OUT

BUS ONLY

BUS STATION

BUS STOP

CAUTION

CLOSED

COMBUSTIBLE

CONDEMNED

CONSTRUCTION

CONTAMINATED

CURVE

DANGER

DANGEROUS CURVE

DEAD END

DEER (CATTLE) CROSSING

DEEP WATER

DENTIST

DETOUR

DIM LIGHTS

DIP

DO NOT BLOCK WALK (DRIVEWAY)

DO NOT CROSS, USE TUNNEL

DO NOT CROWD

DO NOT ENTER

DO NOT INHALE FUMES

DO NOT PUSH

DO NOT REFREEZE

DO NOT SHOVE

DO NOT STAND UP

DO NOT USE NEAR HEAT

DO NOT USE NEAR OPEN FLAME

DOCTOR (DR.)

DON'T WALK

DOWN

DRIFTING SAND

DRIVE SLOW

DYNAMITE

ELEVATOR

EMERGENCY EXIT

EMERGENCY VEHICLES ONLY

EMPLOYEES ONLY

END 45

END CONSTRUCTION

ENTRANCE

EXIT

EXIT ONLY

EXIT SPEED 30

EXPLOSIVES

EXTERNAL USE ONLY

FALLING ROCKS

FALLOUT SHELTER

FIRE ESCAPE

FIRE EXTINGUISHER

FIRST AID

FLAMMABLE

FLOODED

FLOODS WHEN RAINING

FOUND

FOUR WAY STOP

FRAGILE

FREEWAY

GARAGE

GASOLINE

GATE

GENTLEMEN

GO SLOW

HANDLE WITH CARE

HANDS OFF

HELP

HIGH VOLTAGE

HOSPITAL ZONE

IN

INFLAMMABLE

INFORMATION

INSPECTION STATION

INSTRUCTIONS

JUNCTION 101 A

KEEP AWAY

KEEP CLOSED

KEEP OFF (THE GRASS)

KEEP OUT

KEEP TO THE LEFT (RIGHT)

LADIES

LANE ENDS

LAST CHANCE FOR GAS

LEFT LANE MUST TURN LEFT

LEFT TURN ON THIS SIGNAL ONLY

LEFT TURN O.K.

LEFT TURN ONLY

LISTEN

LIVE WIRES

LOADING ZONE

LOOK

LOOK OUT FOR THE CARS (TRUCKS)

LOST

MECHANIC ON DUTY

MEN

MEN WORKING

MERGE LEFT (RIGHT)

MERGING TRAFFIC

MILES PER HOUR (M.P.H.)

MILITARY RESERVATION

NEXT

NEXT WINDOW (GATE)

NO ADMITTANCE

NO CHECKS CASHED

NO CREDIT

NO DIVING

NO DOGS ALLOWED

NO DUMPING

NO FIRES

NO FISHING

NO HUNTING

NO LEFT TURN

NO LOITERING

NO MINORS

NO PARKING

NO PASSING

NO RIGHT TURN

NO RIGHT TURN ON RED LIGHT

NO SMOKING

NO SMOKING AREA

NO SPITTING

NO STANDING

NO STOPPING

NO SWIMMING

NO TOUCHING

NO TRESPASSING

NO TURNS

NO "U" TURNS

NOT A THROUGH STREET

NOT FOR INTERNAL USE

NOXIOUS

NURSE

OFFICE

ONE WAY — DO NOT ENTER

ONE WAY STREET

OPEN

OUT

OUT OF ORDER

PAVEMENT ENDS

PEDESTRIANS PROHIBITED

PED XING

PLAYGROUND

POISON

POISONOUS

POLICE (STATION)

POST NO BILLS

POST OFFICE

POSTED

PRIVATE

PRIVATE PROPERTY

PRIVATE ROAD

PROCEED AT YOUR OWN RISK

PULL

PUSH

PUT ON CHAINS

RAILROAD CROSSING

R.R.

RESTROOMS

RESUME SPEED

RIGHT LANE MUST TURN RIGHT

RIGHT TURN ONLY

ROAD CLOSED

ROAD ENDS

SAFETY FIRST

SCHOOL STOP

SCHOOL ZONE

SHALLOW WATER

SHELTER

SLIDE AREA

SLIPPERY WHEN WET (FROSTY)

SLOW DOWN

SLOWER TRAFFIC KEEP RIGHT

SMOKING PROHIBITED

SPEED CHECKED BY RADAR

STEEP GRADE

STEP DOWN (UP)

STOP

STOP AHEAD

STOP FOR PEDESTRIANS

STOP MOTOR

STOP WHEN OCCUPIED

TAXI STAND

TERMS CASH

THIN ICE

THIS END UP

THIS LANE MAY TURN LEFT

THIS ROAD PATROLLED BY
    AIRCRAFT

THREE WAY LIGHT

TRAFFIC CIRCLE

TRUCK ROUTE

TURN OFF

TURN OFF ½ MILE (¼ MILE)

UNLOADING ZONE

UP

USE BEFORE (DATE)

USE IN OPEN AIR

USE LOW GEAR

USE OTHER DOOR

VIOLATORS WILL BE PROSECUTED

WALK

WANTED

WARNING

WATCH FOR FLAGMAN

WATCH FOR LOW FLYING AIRCRAFT

WATCH YOUR STEP

WET PAINT

WINDING ROAD

WOMEN

YIELD

YIELD RIGHT OF WAY

APPENDIX N
BOOKS FOR
READING ALOUD
TO PRIMARY CHILDREN

PELLE'S NEW SUIT, Elsa Beskow (Harper & Row, 1929)

FIVE CHINESE BROTHERS, Claire H. Bishop (Coward, 1938)

SWITCH ON THE NIGHT, Ray Bradbury (Pantheon, 1955)

JOHNNY CROW'S GARDEN and other *Johnny Crow* books, Leslie Brooke (Watts, 1967)

ONCE A MOUSE, Marcia Brown (Scribner, 1961)

GOODNIGHT MOON, Margaret Wise Brown (Harper & Row, 1977)

LITTLE FUR FAMILY, Margaret Wise Brown (Harper & Row, 1968)

RUNAWAY BUNNY, Margaret Wise Brown (Harper & Row, 1972)

THE WHISPERING RABBIT AND OTHER STORIES, Margaret Wise Brown (Golden Press, 1965)

KATY AND THE BIG SNOW, Virginia Burton (Houghton Mifflin, 1974)

MIKE MULLIGAN, Virginia Burton (Houghton Mifflin, 1977)

WE READ A TO Z, Donald Crews (Harper & Row, 1967)

FLIP, Wesley Dennis (Viking Press, 1941)

A LITTLE HOUSE OF YOUR OWN, Beatrice De Regniers (H. B. & W., 1951)

MAY I BRING A FRIEND?, Beatrice De Regniers (Atheneum, 1964)

PETUNIA books, Roger Duvoisin (Knopf, 1950)

VERONICA books, Roger Duvoisin (Knopf, 1961)

ARE YOU MY MOTHER?, P. D. Eastman (Random House, 1960)

DRUMMER HOFF, Barbara Emberley (Prentice-Hall, 1967)

JUST ME, Marie Hall Ets (Viking Press, 1965)

HAPPY LION books, Louise Fatio (McGraw-Hill, 1954)

THE STORY ABOUT PING, Marjorie Flack (Viking Press, 1933)

ANGUS AND THE DUCKS and other *Angus* books, Marjorie Flack (Doubleday, 1939)

WAIT FOR WILLIAM, Marjorie Flack (Houghton Mifflin, 1961)

ASK MR. BEAR, Marjorie Flack (Macmillan, 1958)

SCAT! SCAT!, Sally Franci (Platt, 1977)

ABC BUNNY, Wanda Gag (Coward-McCann, 1933)

MILLIONS OF CATS, Wanda Gag (Coward-McGann, 1928)

LITTLE TOOT, Hardie Gramatky, (Putnam, 1939)

LITTLE TOOT ON THE THAMES, Hardie Gramatky (Putnam, 1964)

LOOPY, Hardie Gramatky (Putnam, 1941)

A BABY SISTER FOR FRANCES and other *Frances* books, Russell Hoban (Harper & Row, 1964)

A SNOWY DAY, Ezra Keats (Viking Press, 1962)

LETTER TO AMY, Ezra Keats (Harper & Row, 1968)

LITTLE DRUMMER BOY, Ezra Keats (Macmillan, 1968)

PETER'S CHAIR, Ezra Keats (Harper & Row, 1967)

WHISTLE FOR WILLIE, Ezra Keats (Viking Press, 1964)

CHRISTMAS NUTSHELL LIBRARY, Hilary Knight (Harper & Row, 1963)

THE COW WHO FELL IN THE CANAL, Phyllis Krasilovsky (Doubleday, 1972)

THE BUNNY'S NUTSHELL LIBRARY, Robert Kraus (Harper & Row, 1965)

THE STORY OF FERDINAND, Munro Leaf (Viking Press, 1977)

BENJIE, Joan Lexau (Dial Press, 1964)

THEODORE TURTLE, Ellen MacGregor (McGraw-Hill, 1962)

MAKE WAY FOR DUCKLINGS, Robert McCloskey (Viking Press, 1941)

BLUEBERRIES FOR SAL, Robert McCloskey (Viking Press, 1948)

LITTLE BEAR BOOKS, Else Minarik (Harper & Row, 1957)

FINDERS KEEPERS, William Mordvinoff (Harcourt Brace Jovanovich, 1973)

THE ROOSTER CROWS, Maud Petersham (Macmillan, 1945)

THE HAPPY OWLS, Celestino Piatti (Antheneum, 1964)

THE LITTLE ENGINE THAT COULD, Watty Piper (Platt, 1947)

PETER RABBIT, Beatrix Potter (Grosset and Dunlap, 1962)

CURIOUS GEORGE and other *Curious George* books, H. A. Rey (Houghton Mifflin, 1941)

TALL BOOK OF NURSERY TALES, Feodor Rojankovsky (Harper & Row, 1944)

CASEY JONES: THE STORY OF A BRAVE ENGINEER, Glenn Rounds (Golden Gate, 1968)

NUTSHELL LIBRARY, Maurice Sendak (Harper & Row, 1962)

WHERE THE WILD THINGS ARE, Maurice Sendak (Harper & Row, 1963)

HORTON HATCHES THE EGG, Dr. Seuss (Random House, 1940)

CAPS FOR SALE, Esphyr Slobodkin (W. R. Scott, 1947)

FOX WENT OUT ON A CHILLY NIGHT, Peter Spier (Doubleday, 1967)

ANATOLE BOOKS, Eve Titus (McGraw-Hill, 1956)

WHITE SNOW, BRIGHT SNOW, Alvin Tresselt (Lothrop, 1947)

A TREE IS NICE, Janice Udry (Harper & Row, 1956)

CRICTOR, Tomi Ungerer (Harper & Row, 1969)

LYLE, LYLE, CROCODILE and other *Lyle* books, Bernard Waber (Houghton Mifflin, 1973)

THE HOUSE ON EAST 88TH STREET, Bernard Waber (Houghton Mifflin, 1962)

THE BIGGEST BEAR, Lynd Ward (Houghton Mifflin, 1958)

THREE BEDTIME STORIES, Garth Williams (Golden Press, 1958)

UMBRELLA, Taro Yashima (Viking Press, 1977)

BIG BOOKS OF AIRPLANES, George Zaffo (Grosset and Dunlap, 1971)

BIG BOOKS OF REAL FIRE ENGINES, George Zaffo (Grosset and Dunlap, 1973)

BIG BOOKS OF BUILDING AND WRECKING, George Zaffo (Grosset and Dunlap, 1970)

BIG BOOKS OF MACHINES, George Zaffo (Grosset and Dunlap, 1969)

BIG BOOKS OF TRAINS, George Zaffo (Grosset and Dunlap, 1970)

BIG BOOKS OF SHIPS, George Zaffo (Grosset and Dunlap, 1972)

MOMMY BUY ME A CHINA DOLL, Harve Zemach, (Farrar, 1966)

HARRY, THE DIRTY DOG and other *Harry* books, Gene Zion (Harper & Row, 1976)

ALL FALLING DOWN, Gene Zion (Harper & Row, 1951)

APPENDIX O
BOOKS FOR
READING ALOUD
TO THIRD AND
FOURTH GRADERS

MR. POPPER'S PENGUINS, Richard Atwater (Little-Brown, 1938)

MISS HICKORY, Carolyn S. Bailey (Viking, 1946)

CINDERELLA, Marcia Brown (Scribner, 1954)

ONCE A MOUSE, Marcia Brown (Scribner, 1961)

THE STEADFAST TIN SOLDIER, Marcia Brown (Scribner, 1953)

THE WILD SWANS, Marcia Brown (Scribner, 1965)

THE WHITE BIRD, Clyde R. Bulla (Crowell, 1966)

THE FAMILY UNDER THE BRIDGE, Natalie Carlson (Harper, 1972)

HENRY HUGGINS and other *Henry Huggins* books, Beverly Cleary (Morrow, 1960)

THE COLUMBUS STORY, Alice Dalgliesh (Scribner, 1955)

THE COURAGE OF SARAH NOBLE, Alice Dalgliesh (Scribner, 1954)

THE FOURTH OF JULY STORY, Alice Dalgliesh (Scribner, 1952)

THE THANKSGIVING STORY, Alice Dalgliesh (Scribner, 1954)

DANIEL BOONE, James Daugherty (Viking Press, 1939)

THE WHEEL ON THE SCHOOL, Meindert DeJong (Harper & Row, 1954)

THE ALLIGATOR CASE, William Pene du Bois (Harper & Row, 1965)

THE MATCHLOCK GUN, Walter D. Edmonds (Dodd Mead, 1941)

THE HUNDRED DRESSES, Eleanor Estes (Harcourt Brace Jovanovich, 1974)

HITTY, HER FIRST HUNDRED YEARS, Rachel Field (Macmillan, 1937)

OLD YELLER, Fred Gipson (Harper, 1966)

BRIGHTY OF THE GRAND CANYON, Marguerite Henry (Rand McNally, 1953)

MISTY OF CHINCOTEAGUE, Marguerite Henry (Rand McNally, 1947)

SEA STAR, Marguerite Henry (Rand McNally, 1977)

RABBIT HILL, Robert Lawson (Viking Press, 1944)

THE TOUGH WINTER, Robert Lawson (Viking Press, 1954)

PIPPI LONGSTOCKING, Astrid Lindgren (Viking Press, 1950)

LENTIL, Robert McCloskey (Viking Press, 1940)

MISS PICKERELL GOES TO MARS and other *Miss Pickerell* books, Ellen McGregor (McGraw-Hill, 1951)

MISSISSIPPI POSSUM, Miksa Miles (Little-Brown, 1965)

THE BORROWERS and other *Borrowers* books, Mary Norton (Harcourt Brace Jovanovich, 1953)

CRICKET IN TIMES SQUARE, George Selden (Farrar Straus & Giroux, 1960)

CHARLOTTE'S WEB, E. B. White (Harper & Row, 1952)

STUART LITTLE, E. B. White (Harper & Row, 1945)

BY THE SHORES OF SILVER LAKE, Laura Ingalls Wilder (Harper & Row, 1953)

FARMER BOY, Laura Ingalls Wilder (Harper & Row, 1953)

LITTLE HOUSE IN THE BIG WOODS, Laura Ingalls Wilder (Harper & Row, 1953)

LITTLE HOUSE ON THE PRAIRIE, Laura Ingalls Wilder (Harper & Row, 1953)

ON THE BANKS OF PLUM CREEK, Laura Ingalls Wilder (Harper & Row, 1953)

DANNY DUNN AND THE HOMEWORK MACHINE and other *Danny Dunn* books, Joy Williams (McGraw-Hill, 1965)

APPENDIX P
GREAT QUOTATIONS
ON BOOKS AND READING

There is no frigate like a book
To take us lands away.

—Emily Dickinson

Oh for a book and a shady nook.

—John Wilson

My book and heart
Must never part.

—*New England Primer*

A good book is the precious life-blood of a master-spirit.

—John Milton

'Tis the reader that makes the good book.

—Ralph Waldo Emerson

A good book is the best of friends, the same today and forever.

—Martin Tupper

Man builds no structure which outlives a book.

—Eugene Fitch Ware

What a sense of security in an old book which Time has criticized for us!

—James Russell Lowell

"What is the use of a book," thought Alice, "without pictures or conversations?"

—Lewis Carroll

Some books are to be tasted, others to be swallowed, and some few to be chewed and digested.

—Francis Bacon

Books, the children of the brain.

—Jonathan Swift

Life being very short, and the quiet hours of it few, we ought to waste none of them in reading valueless books.

—Jonathan Swift

All books are divisible into two classes: the books of the hour, and the books of all time.

—John Ruskin

The peace of great books be with you.

—Carl Sandburg

Reading great books whets but never slakes the thirst for greatness.

—J. Frank Dobie

Books think for me.

—Charles Lamb

When others fail him, the wise man looks
To the sure companionship of books.

—Andrew Lang

Books are the ever-burning lamps of accumulated wisdom.

—G. W. Curtis

How many a man has dated a new era in his life from the reading of a book?

—Henry David Thoreau

Book love, my friends, is your pass to the greatest, the purest, and the most perfect pleasure that God has prepared for His creatures.

—Anthony Trollope

I go to books and to nature as a bee goes to the flower, for nectar that I can make into my own honey.

—John Burroughs

Live always in the best company when you read.

—Sydney Smith

He was a one-book man. Some men have only one book in them; others, a library.
—Sydney Smith

Reading maketh a full man.

—Francis Bacon

APPENDIX Q

ONE HUNDRED
CREATIVE ALTERNATIVES
TO WRITTEN BOOK REPORTS

1. Prepare a book or story for readers theatre.
2. Write a personality sketch of a book character.
3. Decorate a classroom door to look like a book jacket.
4. Make a felt and burlap wall hanging of a book scene.
5. Construct a table-top village representing a book scene.
6. Create tissue paper "stained-glass windows" showing book characters.
7. Debate the pros and cons of an issue from literature.
8. Compose a folk song about a story character or event.
9. Embroider quilt squares with symbols from favorite books.
10. Demonstrate a procedure from a how-to-do-it book.
11. Decorate wastebaskets and storage boxes with storybook scenes.
12. Conduct a used-book auction.
13. Prepare a classroom rating chart for library books.
14. Select poetry for choral reading.
15. Compile a scrapbook of student book reviews.
16. Prepare stories for reading aloud to younger children.
17. Collect magazine pictures and use them to illustrate favorite poems.
18. Construct a mobile of book characters.
19. Wear sandwich-board posters to promote a book.
20. Write a letter to a publisher and give your impression of a new book.

21. Rewrite an old story as a modern soap opera.
22. Make a frieze to illustrate a narrative poem.
23. Write a newspaper advertisement for a favorite book.
24. Develop a series of crossword puzzles based on popular books.
25. Plan a cooking activity to accompany a book about food.
26. Create an alphabet book with each letter representing a book character.
27. Make an illustrated time line of important events in a book that is historical.
28. Compile a scrapbook about an author, poet, or illustrator.
29. Use a comic-strip format to depict episodes in a story.
30. Make a collection of travel brochures and postcards to illustrate a travel book.
31. Arrange a display of artifacts to accompany a book.
32. Use an opaque projector to show illustrations in a picture book.
33. Paint life-size book characters. Begin by having a friend lie on a large sheet of paper while you trace around his or her figure.
34. Use colored chalk to create a chalk talk about a book.
35. Construct a flip chart depicting scenes from a book.
36. Rewrite a book as a radio play with sound effects and music.
37. Set up a display of old textbooks and library books.
38. Compare an easy-to-read textbook with an easy-to-read trade book.
39. Take a survey to determine which books are favorites throughout the school and set up a display of the winners.
40. Demonstrate some of the art techniques used in Caldecott Award books.
41. Prepare a Book of the Week display.
42. Compare two or more biographies of the same person.
43. Cooperate with a local bookstore to arrange a book fair for the school.
44. Arrange a display of familiar books written in different languages.
45. Make a cumulative book review by collecting sentence comments from students as each finishes a book.
46. Construct advertising posters to promote favorite books.
47. Arrange a hobby collection to promote a book on collecting.
48. Create poster-board bookmarks and illustrate them with storybook scenes.
49. Make a book report in one of the silent languages—signing, finger spelling, or pantomine.
50. Make a chart of figurative language found in a book.
51. Create humorous newspaper headlines and apply them to book characters.

52. Conduct a quiz show similar to "What's My Line?" and have students portray book characters as contestants.

53. Conduct a panel discussion on the themes in popular books.

54. Locate the settings of travel books on a world map.

55. Write an original poem to summarize a book.

56. Rewrite a book as a play and stage it for another class.

57. Conduct a quiz show similar to "I've Got a Secret" and use the secrets of book characters.

58. Dramatize a book, or a scene, in a puppet play.

59. Play Bingo by matching books and authors.

60. Make a new jacket for a book and write a blurb about it.

61. Compare and contrast two books.

62. Compare and contrast two book characters.

63. Compare and contrast two authors.

64. Compare and contrast two illustrators.

65. Draw and cut out storybook characters for the felt board.

66. Prepare a paper scroll using scenes from a story.

67. Construct a shadow box with a storybook scene.

68. Write a new ending to an old story.

69. Dress in costume as book characters and have a parade.

70. Create paper mosaics of story scenes.

71. Model book characters from clay or papier-mâché.

72. Paint a poster of a story scene.

73. Build a structure as described in a how-to-do-it book.

74. Write a newspaper article about a story episode.

75. Plan storytelling sessions for younger children.

76. Prepare a literature newsletter.

77. Role play with familiar book characters.

78. Prepare Monopoly-type board games using book clues.

79. Conduct a panel discussion on science fiction books.

80. Organize a scavenger hunt using book clues.

81. Use magazine advertisements to make a collage of a book scene.

82. Write a letter of recommendation for a well-liked book.

83. Carve story characters from bars of soap.

84. Write an imaginary letter from one character in a book to another.

85. Dress dolls in costume to create a storybook family.

86. Write an additional chapter to a book.
87. Make place mats of book scenes and laminate the mats for table use.
88. Compile an imaginary diary as it might have been kept by a book character.
89. Tape-record a book report and play it for the class.
90. Write an imaginary autobiography of a book character.
91. Interview another student who is impersonating the main character from a biography or autobiography.
92. Make a collection of famous quotations from literature and post them on the bulletin board.
93. Make a comparative study of children's classics and rate them on a bar graph.
94. Exchange a series of letters with a pen pal in which books are the main topic of discussion.
95. Select a holiday; and at the appropriate time, set up an exhibit of books suitable for holiday reading.
96. Make a collection of poems on various themes.
97. Illustrate an oral book report with taped excerpts from the book.
98. Write a television commercial advertising a favorite book.
99. Write an essay entitled "The Wisest Book I Have Ever Known" and share it with the class.
100. Plan a literature program to be performed for parents, teachers, and students.

APPENDIX R
THE CALDECOTT AWARD BOOKS

1938 *Animals of the Bible*, by Helen Dean Fish, illustrated by Dorothy O. Lathrop (Lippincott)
1939 *Mei Li* by Thomas Handforth (Doubleday)
1940 *Abraham Lincoln* by Ingri d' Aulaire and Edgar Parin d' Aulaire (Doubleday)
1941 *They Were Strong and Good* by Robert Lawson (Viking Press)
1942 *Make Way for Ducklings* by Robert McCloskey (Viking Press)

1943 *The Little House* by Virginia Lee Burton (Houghton Mifflin)

1944 *Many Moons* by James Thurber, illustrated by Louis Slobodkin (Harcourt Brace Jovanovich)

1945 *Prayer for a Child* by Rachel Field, illustrated by Elizabeth Orton Jones (Macmillan)

1946 *The Rooster Crows* by Maud Petersham and Miska Petersham (Macmillan)

1947 *The Little Island* by Golden MacDonald, illustrated by Leonard Weisgard (Doubleday)

1948 *White Snow, Bright Snow* by Alvin Tresselt, illustrated by Roger Duvoisin (Lothrop)

1949 *The Big Snow* by Berta Hader and Elmer Hader (Macmillan)

1950 *Song of the Swallows* by Leo Politi (Scribner)

1951 *The Egg Tree* by Katherine Milhous (Scribner)

1952 *Finders Keepers* by William Lipkind, illustrated by Nicolas Mordvinoff (Harcourt Brace Jovanovich)

1953 *The Biggest Bear* by Lynd Ward (Houghton Mifflin)

1954 *Madeline's Rescue* by Ludwig Bemelmans (Viking Press)

1955 *Cinderella* by Charles Perrault, illustrated by Marcia Brown, (Scribner)

1956 *Frog Went A-Courtin'* by John Langstaff, illustrated by Feodor Rojankovsky (Harcourt Brace Jovanovich)

1957 *A Tree Is Nice* by Janice May Udry, illustrated by Marc Simont (Harper & Row)

1958 *Time of Wonder* by Robert McCloskey (Viking Press)

1959 *Chanticleer and the Fox*, edited and illustrated by Barbara Cooney (Crowell)

1960 *Nine Days to Christmas* by Marie Hall Ets and Aurora Labastida (Viking Press)

1961 *Baboushka and the Three Kings* by Ruth Robbins, illustrated by Nicholas Sidjakov (Parnassus)

1962 *Once a Mouse* by Marcia Brown (Scribner)

1963 *The Snowy Day* by Ezra Jack Keats (Viking Press)

1964 *Where the Wild Things Are* by Maurice Sendak (Harper & Row)

1965 *May I Bring a Friend?* by Beatrice Schenk de Regniers, illustrated by Beni Montresor (Atheneum)

1966 *Always Room for One More* by Sorche Nic Leodhas, illustrated by Nonny Hogrogian (Holt, Rinehart and Winston)

1967 *Sam, Bangs and Moonshine* by Evaline Ness (Holt, Rinehart and Winston)

1968 *Drummer Hoff* by Barbara Emberley, illustrated by Ed Emberley (Prentice-Hall)

1969 *The Fool of the World and the Flying Ship* by Arthur Ransome, illustrated by Uri Shulevitz (Farrar, Straus & Giroux)

1970 *Sylvester and the Magic Pebble* by William Steig (Windmill Books)

1971 *A Story—A Story* by Gail E. Haley (Atheneum)

1972 *One Fine Day* by Nonny Hogrogian (Macmillan)

1973 *The Funny Little Woman* by Arlene Mosel, illustrated by Blair Lent (Dutton)

1974 *Duffy and the Devil* by Harve Zemach, illustrated by Margot Zemach (Farrar, Straus & Giroux)

1975 *Arrow to the Sun*, adapted and illustrated by Gerald McDermott (Viking Press)

1976 *Why Mosquitoes Buzz in People's Ears* by Verna Aardema, illustrated by Leo Dillon and Diane Dillon (Dial Press)

1977 *Ashanti to Zulu: African Traditions* by Margaret Musgrove, illustrated by Leo Dillon and Diane Dillon (Dial Press)

1978 *Noah's Ark* by Peter Spier (Doubleday)

1979 *The Girl Who Loved Wild Horses*, by Paul Goble (Bradbury Press)

1980 *Ox-Cart Man* by Donald Hall, illustrated by Barbara Cooney (Viking Press)

1981 *Fables* by Arnold Lobel (Harper & Row)

APPENDIX S
THE NEWBERY
AWARD BOOKS

1922 *The Story of Mankind* by Hendrik Van Loon (Liveright)

1923 *The Voyages of Doctor Dolittle* by Hugh Lofting (Lippincott)

1924 *The Dark Frigate* by Charles Boardman Hawes (Little, Brown)

1925 *Tales from Silver Lands,* by Charles J. Finger (Doubleday)

1926 *Shen of the Sea* by Arthur Bowie Chrisman (Dutton)

1927 *Smoky, the Cowhorse* by Will James (Scribner)

1928 *Gay-neck, the Story of a Pigeon* by Dhan Gopal Mukerji (Dutton)

1929 *The Trumpeter of Krakow* by Eric P. Kelly (Macmillan)

1930 *Hitty, Her First Hundred Years* by Rachel Field (Macmillan)

1931 *The Cat Who Went to Heaven* by Elizabeth Coatsworth (Macmillan)

1932 *Waterless Mountain* by Laura Adams Armer (Longmans)

1933 *Young Fu of the Upper Yangtze* by Elizabeth Foreman Lewis (Holt, Rinehart and Winston)

1934 *Invincible Louisa* by Cornelia Meigs (Little, Brown)

1935 *Dobry* by Monica Shannon (Viking Press)

1936 *Caddie Woodlawn* by Carol Ryrie Brink (Macmillan)

1937 *Roller Skates* by Ruth Sawyer (Viking Press)

1938 *The White Stag* by Kate Seredy (Viking Press)

1939 *Thimble Summer* by Elizabeth Enright (Holt, Rinehart and Winston)

1940 *Daniel Boone* by James H. Daugherty (Viking Press)

1941 *Call It Courage* by Armstrong Sperry (Macmillan)

1942 *The Matchlock Gun* by Walter D. Edmonds (Dodd, Mead)

1943 *Adam of the Road* by Elizabeth Janet Gray (Viking Press)

1944 *Johnny Tremain* by Esther Forbes (Houghton Mifflin)

1945 *Rabbit Hill* by Robert Lawson (Viking Press)

1946 *Strawberry Girl* by Lois Lenski (Lippincott)

1947 *Miss Hickory* by Carolyn Sherwin Bailey (Viking Press)

1948 *The Twenty-One Balloons* by William Pene du Bois (Viking Press)

1949 *King of the Wind* by Marguerite Henry (Rand McNally)

1950 *The Door in the Wall* by Marguerite de Angeli (Doubleday)

1951 *Amos Fortune, Free Man* by Elizabeth Yates (Dutton)

1952 *Ginger Pye* by Eleanor Estes (Harcourt Brace Jovanovich)

1953 *Secret of the Andes* by Ann Nolan Clark (Viking Press)

1954 *. . . and now Miguel* by Joseph Krumgold (Crowell)

1955 *The Wheel on the School* by Meindert DeJong (Harper & Row)

1956 *Carry On, Mr. Bowditch* by Jean Lee Latham (Houghton Mifflin)

1957 *Miracles on Maple Hill* by Virginia Sorensen (Harcourt Brace Jovanovich)

1958 *Rifles for Waite* by Harold Keith (Crowell)

1959 *The Witch of Blackbird Pond* by Elizabeth George Speare (Houghton Mifflin)

1960 *Onion John* by Joseph Krumgold (Crowell)

1961 *Island of the Blue Dolphins* by Scott O'Dell (Houghton Mifflin)

1962 *The Bronze Bow* by Elizabeth George Speare (Houghton Mifflin)

1963 *A Wrinkle in Time* by Madeleine L'Engle (Farrar, Straus & Giroux)

1964 *It's Like This, Cat* by Emily Neville (Harper & Row)

1965 *Shadow of a Bull* by Maia Wojciechowska (Atheneum)

1966 *I, Juan de Pareja* by Elizabeth Borton de Trevino (Farrar, Straus & Giroux)

1967 *Up a Road Slowly* by Irene Hunt (Follett)

1968 *From the Mixed-Up Files of Mrs. Basil E. Frankweiler* by E. L. Konigsburg (Atheneum)

1969 *The High King* by Lloyd Alexander (Holt, Rinehart and Winston)

1970 *Sounder* by William H. Armstrong (Harper & Row)

1971 *The Summer of the Swans* by Betsy Byars (Viking Press)

1972 *Mrs. Frisby and the Rats of NIMH* by Robert C. O'Brien (Atheneum)

1973 *Julie of the Wolves* by Jean Craighead George (Harper & Row)

1974 *The Slave Dancer* by Paula Fox (Bradbury Press)

1975 *M. C. Higgins, the Great* by Virginia Hamilton (Macmillan)

1976 *The Grey King* by Susan Cooper (Atheneum)

1977 *Roll of Thunder, Hear My Cry* by Mildred D. Taylor (Dial Press)

1978 *Bridge to Terabithia* by Katherine Paterson (Crowell)

1979 *The Westing Game* by Ellen Raskin (Dutton)

1980 *A Gathering of Days* by Joan W. Blos (Scribner)

1981 *Jacob Have I Loved* by Katherine Paterson (Crowell)

APPENDIX T
PUBLISHERS' ADDRESSES

Abelard-Schuman Ltd.
10 E. 53rd St.
New York, N.Y. 10022

Abingdon Press
201 Eighth Ave. S.
Nashville, Tenn. 37202

Addison-Wesley Publishing co., Inc.
Reading, Mass. 01867

Allyn & Bacon, Inc.
470 Atlantic Avenue
Boston, Mass. 02210

American Book Co.
135 W. 50th St.
New York, N.Y. 10020

American Education Publications
1250 Fairwood Ave.
Columbus, Ohio 43216

American Heritage Publishing
    Co., Inc.
10 Rockefeller Plaza
New York, N.Y. 10020

American Library Association
50 E. Huron St.
Chicago, Ill. 60611

Atheneum Publishers
122 E. 42nd St.
New York, N.Y. 10017

Atherton Press
70 Fifth Avenue
New York, N.Y. 10011

Ballantine Books, Inc.
201 E. South St.
New York, N.Y. 10022

Bantam Books
School and College Division
666 Fifth Ave.
New York, N.Y. 10019

A. S. Barnes & Co., Inc.
Forsgate Dr.
Cranbury, N.J. 08512

Barnes and Noble Books
10 E. 53rd St.
New York, N.Y. 10022

Beacon Press
25 Beacon Street
Boston, Mass. 02108

Beckley-Cardy Co.
1900 N. Narragansett
Chicago, Ill. 60611

Bobbs-Merrill Co., Inc.
4300 West 62nd St.
Indianapolis, Ind. 46206

Bodley Head Ltd.
9 Bow Street
London, England WC2E7AL

R. R. Bowker Co.
1180 Avenue of the Americas
New York, N.Y. 10036

Bowmar, Noble Publishers, Inc.
4563 Colorado Blvd.
Los Angeles, Calif. 90039

Bradbury Press, Inc.
2 Overhill Rd.
Scarsdale, N.Y. 10583

George Braziller, Inc.
1 Park Ave.
New York, N.Y. 10016

Broadman Press
127 Ninth Ave., N.
Nashville, Tenn. 37234

Wm. C. Brown Co., Publishers
2460 Kerper Boulevard
Dubuque, Iowa 52001

Burgess Publishing Co.
7108 Ohms Lane
Minneapolis, Minn. 55435

Cambridge University Press
32 E. 57th St.
New York, N.Y. 10022

Center for Applied Research
   in Education
70 Fifth Ave.
New York, N.Y. 10011

Century House Publishing, Inc.
Watkins Glen, N.Y. 14891

Chandler & Sharp Publishers, Inc.
11A Commerical Blvd.
Novato, Calif. 94947

Children's Book Council
175 Fifth Ave.
New York, N.Y. 10010

Chilton Book Company
Chilton Way
Radnor, Pa. 19089

Citation Press
50 W. 44th St.
New York, N.Y. 10036

Williams Collins Publishers, Inc.
2080 W. 117th St.
Cleveland, Ohio 44111

F. E. Compton Co.
425 N. Michigan Ave.
Chicago, Ill. 60611

Coward, McCann and
    Geoghegan, Inc.
200 Madison Ave.
New York, N.Y. 10016

Cowles Book Co.
488 Madison Ave.
New York, N.Y. 10022

Creative Education, Inc.
123 S. Broad St.
Mankato, Minn. 56001

Criterion Books
666 Fifth Ave.
New York, N.Y. 10019

Crowell-Collier
866 Third Ave.
New York, N.Y. 10022

Thomas Y. Crowell Co., Publishers
666 Fifth Ave.
New York, N.Y. 10019

Crown Publishers, Inc.
1 Park Ave.
New York, N.Y. 10016

John Day Co.
257 Park Ave. S.
New York, N.Y. 10010

Delacorte Press
Dell Publishing Co., Inc.
1 Dag Hammarskjold Plaza
New York, N.Y. 10017

Dial Press
1 Dag Hammerskjold Plaza
New York, N.Y. 10017

Dillon Press, Inc.
500 S. Third St.
Minneapolis, Minn. 55415

Dodd, Mead & Co.
79 Madison Ave.
New York, N.Y. 10016

Doubleday and Co., Inc.
245 Park Ave.
New York, N.Y. 10017

Dover Publications, Inc.
180 Varick St.
New York, N.Y. 10014

Gerald Duckworth & Co., Ltd.
436 Glouster Crescent
London, England NW170V

Dufour Editions, Inc.
Chester Springs, Pa. 19425

E. P. Dutton & Co.
2 Park Ave.
New York, N.Y. 10016

Educational Technology Publications
140 Sylvan Avenue
Englewood Cliffs, N.J. 07632

Encyclopaedia Britannica, Inc.
425 N. Michigan Ave.
Chicago, Ill. 60611

M. Evans and Co., Inc.
216 E. 49th St.
New York, N.Y. 10017

Eye Gate House
146-01 Archer Ave.
Jamaica, N.Y. 10017

Faber and Faber Ltd.
3 Queen Square
London, England WCIN3AV

Farrar, Straus & Giroux, Inc.
19 Union Sq. W.
New York, N.Y. 10003

F. W. Faxon Co., Inc.
15 Southwest Park
Westwood, Mass. 02090

Fearon Pitman Publishers, Inc.
6 Davis Drive
Belmont, Calif. 94002

Field Enterprises Educational Corp.
510 Merchandise Mart Plaza
Chicago, Ill. 60654

Follett Publishing Co.
1010 W. Washington Blvd.
Chicago, Ill. 60607

Four Winds Press
50 W. 44th Street
New York, N.Y. 10021

Franklin Publishing Co.
2047 Locust St.
Philadelphia, Pa. 19103

Free Press
866 Third Ave.
New York, N.Y. 10022

Funk & Wagnalls, Inc.
55 E. 77th St.
New York, N.Y. 10021

Garrard Publishing Co.
1607 N. Market St.
Champaign, Ill. 61820

Ginn and Co.
191 Spring St.
Lexington, Mass. 02173

Golden Gate Junior Books
1224 W. Van Buren St.
Chicago, Ill. 60607

Golden Press
1220 Mound Ave.
Racine, Wis. 53404

Grade Teacher
P. O. Box 225
Cortland, N.Y. 13045

Greenwillow Books
105 Madison Ave.
New York, N.Y. 10016

Grosset and Dunlap, Inc.
51 Madison Ave.
New York, N.Y. 10010

Grossman Publishers
44 W. 56th St.
New York, N.Y. 10019

Hammond, Inc.
515 Valley St.
Maplewood, N.J. 07040

Harcourt Brace Jovanovich, Inc.
757 Third Ave.
New York, N.Y. 10017

Harlin Quist Books
1 Dag Hammarskjold Plaza
New York, N.Y. 10017

Harper & Row, Publishers, Inc.
10 E. 53rd St.
New York, N.Y. 10022

Harvey House, Publishers
20 Waterside Plaza
New York, N.Y. 10010

Hastings House Publishers, Inc.
10 E. 40th St.
New York, N.Y. 10016

Hawthorn Books, Inc.
260 Madison Ave.
New York, N.Y. 10016

D. C. Heath and Co.
125 Spring St.
Lexington, Mass. 02173

Hill & Wang
19 Union Sq. W.
New York, N.Y. 10003

Holbrook Press
470 Atlantic Ave.
Boston, Mass. 02210

Holiday House, Inc.
18 E. 53rd St.
New York, N.Y. 10022

Holt, Rinehart and Winston
383 Madison Ave.
New York, N.Y. 10017

Horn Book, Inc.
Park Square Bldg.
21 St. James Ave.
Boston, Mass. 02116

Houghton Mifflin Co., Inc.
2 Park St.
Boston, Mass. 02107

International Reading Association
P.O. Box 695
Newark, Del. 19711

Island Heritage Ltd.
828 Fort St. Mall
Suite 400
Honolulu, Hawaii 96813

Alfred A. Knopf, Inc.
201 E. 50th St.
New York, N.Y. 10022

Lerner Publications Co.
241 First Ave. N.
Minneapolis, Minn. 55401

Library Association
7 Ridgemount St.
London, England WCIE7AE

Library of Congress
Washington, D.C. 20540

Lion Books
111 E. 39th St.
New York, N.Y. 10016

J. B. Lippincott Co.
521 Fifth Ave.
New York, N.Y. 10017

Little Brown and Co.
34 Beacon St.
Boston, Mass. 02106

Longmans, Green & Co.
55 Fifth Ave.
New York, N.Y. 10003

Lothrop, Lee & Shepard Books
105 Madison Ave.
New York, N.Y. 10016

McCutchan Publishing Corp.
2526 Grove St.
Berkeley, Calif. 94704

McGraw-Hill Book Co.
1221 Avenue of the Americas
New York, N.Y. 10020

David McKay Co., Inc.
2 Park Ave.
New York, N.Y. 10016

McKinley Publishing Co.
P.O. Box 77
Ocean City, N. J. 08226

Macmillan, Inc.
866 Third Ave.
New York, N.Y. 10022

Mentor Press
New American Library
1633 Broadway
New York, N.Y. 10019

Meredith Corp.
1716 Locust St.
Des Moines, Iowa 50336

G. & C. Merriam Co.
47 Federal St.
Springfield, Mass. 01101

Charles E. Merrill Publishing Co.
1300 Alum Creek Dr.
Columbus, Ohio 43216

Julian Messner
1230 Avenue of the Americas
New York, N.Y. 10020

William Morrow & Co., Inc.
105 Madison Ave.
New York, N.Y. 10016

National Council of Teachers of
    English
111 Kenyon Rd.
Urbana, Ill. 61801

National Education Association
    Publishing
1201 16th St., N.W.
Washington, D.C. 20036

Natural History Press
277 Park Ave.
New York, N.Y. 10017

Thomas Nelson, Inc.
407 Seventh Ave. S.
Nashville, Tenn. 37203

New American Library, Inc.
1633 Broadway
New York, N.Y. 10019

New York Graphic Society Books
41 Mt. Vernon St.
Boston, Mass. 02106

W. W. Norton & Co , Inc.
500 Fifth Ave.
New York, N.Y. 10036

Oddo Publishing, Inc.
Storybook Acres
Beauregard Blvd.
Fayetteville, Ga. 30214

F. A. Owen Publishing Co.
Dansville, N.Y. 14437

Oxford University Press, Inc.
200 Madison Ave.
New York, N.Y. 10016

Paddington Press Ltd.
95 Madison Ave.
New York, N.Y. 10016

Palo Verde Publishing Co.
609 N. Fourth Ave.
Tucson, Ariz. 85716

Pantheon Books, Inc.
201 E. 50th St.
New York, N.Y. 10022

Parnassus Press
P.O. Box 8443
Emeryville, Calif. 94608

Parents' Magazine Press
52 Vanderbilt Ave.
New York, N.Y. 10017

Penguin Books, Inc.
625 Madison Ave.
New York, N.Y. 10022

Pergamon Press, Inc.
Maxwell House
Fairview Park
Elmsford, N.Y. 10523

Personalized Reading Center
Xerox Education Center
Columbus, Ohio 43216

Personnel Press
191 Spring St.
Lexington, Mass. 02173

Peter Pauper Press
135 W. 50th St.
New York, N.Y. 10020

S. G. Phillips, Inc.
305 W. 86th St.
New York, N.Y. 10024

Pitman Publishing Co.
6 Davis Dr.
Belmont, Calif. 94002

Platt and Munk Co.
1055 Bronx River Ave.
Bronx, N.Y. 10472

Pocket Books
1230 Avenue of the Americas
New York, N.Y. 10020

Praeger Publishers
521 Fifth Ave.
New York, N.Y. 10007

Prentice-Hall, Inc.
Englewood Cliffs, N. J. 07632

G. P. Putnam's Sons
200 Madison Ave.
New York, N.Y. 10016

Rand McNally & Co.
8255 Central Park Ave.
Skokie, Ill. 60076

Random House, Inc.
201 E. 50th St.
New York, N.Y. 10022

Regnery/Gateway, Inc.
Box 207
South Bend, Ind. 46624

St. Martin's Press, Inc.
175 Fifth Ave.
New York, N.Y. 10010

W. B. Saunders Co.
West Washington Sq.
Philadelphia, Pa. 19105

Scarecrow Press
52 Liberty St.
Metuchen, N. J. 08840

Schocken Books, Inc.
200 Madison Ave.
New York, N.Y. 10016

Scholastic Books, Inc.
200 Madison Ave.
New York, N.Y. 10036

Scholastic Book Services
Scholastic Magazines, Inc.
50 W. 44th St.
New York, N.Y. 10036

Scholastic Productions
Pleasantville, N.Y. 10570

Science Research Associates
155 N. Wacker Dr.
Chicago, Ill. 60606

Scott, Foresman & Co.
1900 E. Lake Avenue
Glenview, Ill. 60025

Charles Scribner's Sons
597 Fifth Ave.
New York N.Y. 10017

Scroll Press, Inc.
559 W. 26th St.
New York, N.Y. 10001

Seabury Press, Inc.
815 Second Ave.
New York, N.Y. 10017

Silver Burdett Co.
250 James St.
Morristown, N. J. 07960

Signet Books
New American Library, Inc.
1633 Broadway
New York, N.Y. 10019

Simon and Schuster, Inc.
1230 Avenue of the Americas
New York, N.Y. 10020

Stackpole Books
Cameron and Kelker Sts.
Harrisburg, Pa. 17105

Sterling Publishing Co., Inc.
2 Park Ave.
New York, N.Y. 10016

Taplinger Publishing Co.
200 Park Ave.
New York, N.Y. 10003

Teachers College Press
Columbia University
1234 Amsterdam Ave.
New York, N.Y. 10027

Time-Life Books, Inc.
Alexandria, Va. 22314

Tudor Publishing Co.
31 W. 46th St.
New York, N.Y. 10036

Charles E. Tuttle Co., Inc.
28 S. Main St.
Rutland, Vt. 05701

U. S. Government Printing Office
Washington, D.C. 20401

Van Nostrand Reinhold Co.
135 W. 50th St.
New York, N.Y. 10020

Vanguard Press, Inc.
424 Madison Ave.
New York, N.Y. 10017

Viking Press
625 Madison Ave.
New York, N.Y. 10022

Henry Z. Walck, Inc.
2 Park Ave.
New York, N.Y. 10016

Walker and Co.
720 Fifth Ave.
New York, N.Y. 10019

Frederick Warne & Co., Inc.
2 Park Ave.
New York, N.Y. 10016

Washington Square Press
1230 Avenue of the Americas
New York, N.Y. 10020

Watson-Guptill Publications
1515 Broadway
New York, N.Y. 10036

Franklin Watts, Inc.
730 Fifth Ave.
New York, N.Y. 10019

Western Publishing Co., Inc.
1220 Mound Ave.
Racine, Wis. 53404

Westminster Press
925 Chestnut St.
Philadelphia, Pa. 19107

David White, Inc.
14 Vanderventer Ave.
Port Washington, N.Y. 11050

Albert Whitman & Co.
560 West Lake St.
Chicago, Ill. 60606

John Wiley & Sons, Inc.
605 Third Ave.
New York, N.Y. 10016

Windmill Books, Inc.
1230 Avenue of the Americas
New York, N.Y. 10020

Xerox Educational Publications
245 Long Hill Rd.
Middletown, Conn. 06457

Yale University Press
302 Temple St.
New Haven, Conn. 06511

Young Scott Books
Addison-Wesley Publishing Co., Inc.
Reading, Mass. 01867